PALO MAYOMBE

SPIRITS - RITUALS - SPELLS

PALO MAYOMBE - PALO MONTE - KIMBISA

AMERICAN CANDOMBLE CHURCH PUBLICATIONS, LOS ANGELES

PALO MAYOMBE

SPIRITS - RITUALS - SPELLS

PALO MAYOMBE - PALO MONTE - KIMBISA

AMERICAN CANDOMBLE CHURCH
P.O. BOX 881377
LOS ANGELES, CALIFORNIA 90009

LEGAL DISCLAIMER

No part of this book may be reproduced in any manner without written permission from the publisher or the author of this book. This book contains formulas that were used in the historical AFRO-CARIBBEAN religious practices of Santeria, Palo Mayombe, Palo Monte and Kimbisa. The author and the publisher do not encourage any of the practices in this book nor do we assume any liabilities for presenting those formulas in this book. The formulas are presented for curious only. Neither the author nor the publisher, American Candomble Church assumes any responsibilities for the outcome of any of the spells, rituals or initiations in this book. We make no claims to any supernatural powers of these traditional initiation rituals. All inquiries or comments may be directed to the publisher. Warning: please be advised that all of the human bones and many of the animals used in these traditional magic formulas are available through biological supply distributors, taxidermy stores, zoos and museum stores. All of these items are available for sale on ebay. Grave digging, grave robbing and the use of endangered animals is illegal. Individuals must check with their individual state agencies and federal regulations to see if laws prohibit animal sacrifice, buying or selling of Human Bones and endangered animals. To investigate the legalities of animal sacrifice please refer to the Legal Case of *"Hialeah vs. The Church of Lucumi"* which established Santeria as a legitimate religion in the United States of America. You must be at least 18 years of age or older to purchase this book or to purchase any of the supplies listed herein.

TABLE OF CONTENTS

INTRODUCTION TO CONGO RELIGION

The Congo Spirits of the dead who make a pact with the living are collectively called "*Nkisi*". The spirits come from the World of the Dead and manifest through the Nganga. The Nganga is usually constructed inside of a cast iron caldron or even inside of a clay pot. The Nganga is a miniature world and doorway to the supernatural. The Nganga is the home of the Nkisi (Congo Spirit) who rests inside waiting until summoned by its owner. The spirit can only manifest to its owner who has made an eternal pact with the World of the Spirits of Darkness that will last until the physical death of its owner. The purpose of the spirit is to serve and protect its master by any means necessary. In the World of the Congo Spirits, good and evil are looked upon equally and weighed the same. That is, there is no distinct classification between good and evil as the Western World believes. Where do these spirits come from and why are they here? There are spirits everywhere around us. Everything, location and thing found in this world and the cosmos contain some kind of spiritual energy and life force. There are pantheons of spiritual entities known as "restless spirits" that for some reason have not been able to pass through light dimensions and are trapped here inside of our world until they complete their task or their destiny. There are many different types of spiritual entities which exist and can be found in the mountains, forest, stones, trees, rivers, oceans and other far away locations such as the planets and the stars. Spirits are pure unseen and invisible energy that can manifest in our physical world. Through the use of ancient magical necromancy incantations and ancient magical sorcery formulas and preparations an individual can tap into this energy and stabilize it by undergoing a series of initiations into this mysterious world which will allow them to walk with authority and respect in the realm of the spirits. In the African Congo religious tradition of spirituality, initiations and pacts with the spirits are achieved through a series of very ancient initiations that link the physical dimension which we live in with the outer dimension, where the spirits reside. These initiations were restricted to a hierarchy of select individuals who would honor the traditions, culture and customs of a proud African Congo people. When an individual undergoes the ancient initiation process these invisible spiritual entities will then recognize the new initiate as one of their own and in return will give the individual access to the secret "Cosmic Keys" to unlock the forbidden doors of the "Universal Occult Mysteries". The scientific study of how these invisible spirits manifest within our physical world through the use of ancient necromancy invocations is called "Occult Physics". The science of "Occult Physics" is the study of an unknown or invisible matter and its motion through space time and all that derives from these, such as energy and force. More broadly, it is the general analysis of how these unseen invisible forces react in nature, conducted in or-der to understand how the world and universe behave. The techniques of how to capture spirits and to harness their strange and very powerful energy to do ones bidding is commonplace in all ancient cultures but the method by which an individual accomplished this varies from culture to culture and from region to region. In Western and European culture individuals initiated into the Spiritual Mysteries were many of times referred to as Witches, Warlocks and Sorcerers. In the African Congo religious tradition they are known as Mayomberos. The word Mayombero refers to an individual who possesses great "occult knowledge" and supernatural power to invoke, summon and to command the spirits of the dead for a variety of reasons such as to heal individuals from disease, sickness, power and protection against the evil eye and entities more commonly known as demons. The practice of working with the spirits of the dead is called necromancy. King Solomon, one of the greatest and most famous individuals of world biblical history was a sorcerer as well as a necromancer. After the African Diaspora to the New World (Trans-Atlantic Slave Trade), these initiations remained almost intact with a few variations and some syncretism and the incorporation of indigenous Indian and Christian elements.

The following text is a historical documentation of some magical formulas and sacred rituals that link and connect the physical world with the sacred and the divine. It is a very strange world that many modern day scientists acknowledge but have not been able to fully explain. This world can only be reached, explained and experienced by direct initiation and participation. These sacred and magical formulas are used in the Caribbean by practitioners from the Afro-Congo religious sect known as Palo Mayombe, Palo Monte and Kimbisa. Although the nganga formulas will vary from region or country, they are all derived from the same tribes of the African Congo. The various forms of Congo religion found in the New World have adapted and have successfully incorporated and are composed of a vast pantheon of spiritual deities, spirits, angels and demons. The following Congo initiation spirit formulas presented here in this book are fundamental base spiritual formulas. Over a period of time of working with the spirits, they may request more items and ingredients that can be added at a later time. An experienced Mayombero Priest (Caribbean) will be able to determine this at the time of preparing the Congo Spirit Nganga or before doing an initiation. Depending on the Congo religious tradition or mystic school that you belong to, the following sacred formulas can be modified to fit your specific needs. All of the spirits presented here in this book can be found in many ancient cultures, but are known by other names and are venerated and magically manifested differently. The following Congo initiation formula is about how to prepare and present the Congo Spiritual Nganga more commonly known as the "*Caldero Espiritual*" (Spiritual Cauldron). All of the following Latin American Necromancy Initiation rituals are authentic and will be discussed in detail about how to correctly perform these very delicate initiation rituals. Depending on the Congo tradition that you belong to, it can be modified to fit your religious traditions specific needs. All of the formulas presented here in this book are real and authentic.

A picture of the "Palma Real" tree. The Palma Real tree is used by Congo Priests to summon the Congo Spirits for magical spiritual work. The spiritual work is usually left at the foot of this very powerful spirit tree along with traditional offerings.

THE CONGO PANTHEON OF GODS

The Congo spirits venerated by initiates of the Afro-Caribbean religious initiates of Palo Mayombe, Palo Monte and Kimbiza are collectively referred to as the "'Mpungu". These spirits are also referred to as "Nkisi" when referring to them in singular form. The sacred magical mysteries of these Nkisi spirits are traditional found and presented to initiates of the Congo religious tradition in a sacred vessel referred to as the Nganga. There is a structured religious hierarchy of the spirits found within the Congo religious tradition. This religious hierarchy is divided between two spiritual realms known as the Greater Congo Spirits (Gods) and the Lesser Congo Spirits (Gods). The Lesser Congo Spirits are subordinate to the deities of the Greater Congo Spirits. The deities found within the realm of the Lesser Congo Spirits represent aspects of nature, such as thunder, agriculture and wind. The highest level of the Congo religious pantheon is occupied by the Creator God, Nzambi.

GREATER CONGO SPIRIT KINGDOMS

NZAMBI

Nzambi is not an actual Mpungu, but a Higher God, the Creator of the Universe and the Cosmos. All of the Congo Spirits of the Lesser Congo Spirit realm are subordinate to him.

LUKANKANSE

The negative aspect of Nzambi, in many ways similar to the Christian Devil.

LESSER CONGO SPIRIT KINGDOMS

LUCERO

The Nkisi Spirit, Lucero is the grand guardian of the Crossroads. This Congo Spirit represents spiritual guidance and spiritual balance. He also represents spiritual communication between humans and the spirit world. Each of the Congo Spirits found within the Lesser Congo Spirit realm has its own unique guardian Lucero spirit that walks with each of them. The primary Lucero found within the Afro-Caribbean Congo religion is called, Lucero Vira Mundo. The Spirit Lucero Vira Mundo is the father of all of the other spiritual paths of Lucero found within the Lesser Congo Spirit Kingdoms.

KOBAYENDE

The Nkisi Spirit, Kobayende is the guardian of diseases and sickness. He is the guardian of the cemetery gates.

CENTELLA NDOKI

The Nkisi Spirit, Centella Ndoki is the guardian of all events between life and death. She is also guardian of the winds and of the cemetery.

GURUNFINDA

The Nkisi Spirit, Gurunfinda is the guardian of the forest and sacred magical herbs. This spirit is also called by initiates of the Afro-Caribbean Congo religion as "Ozain".

MADRE DE AGUA

The Nkisi Spirit, Madre De Agua is the guardian of the oceans and of fertility. She represents purification, peace, harmony of home and balance of the element of Earth.

CALUNGA

The Nkisi Spirit, Calunga is the guardian of the mysteries of ocean's depths. Calunga is also the keeper of the secrets of wealth found at the bottom of the ocean and the guardian of all souls of individuals who lost their lives at sea.

MAMA SHOLAN

The Nkisi Spirit, Mama Sholan is the guardian of the rivers, love and wealth. Mama Sholan is also invoked and summoned to bring individuals together for marriage.

TIEMPO VIEJO

The Nkisi Spirit, Tiempo Viejo (Father Time) is the guardian of sacred divination. Tiempo Viejo knows our past, present and our future.

CABO RONDO

The Nkisi Spirit, Cabo Rondo is the guardian of social justice and all legal matters. Cabo Rondo can also be invoked and summoned to protect an individual from going to jail.

SIETE RAYOS

The Nkisi Spirit, Siete Rayos is the guardian of thunder, fire and lightning. Siete Rayos can also be invoked and summoned to triumph over all enemies known and unknown. Siete Rayos can also be called upon in matters of love and dominating a particular individual for romance.

TIEMBLA TIERRA

The Nkisi Spirit, Tiembla Tierra is the guardian of sacred wisdom and divine justice. Tiembla Tierra can be invoked and summoned for all legal and court matters. Tiembla Tierra also brings calmness, harmony and self-tranquility to our minds and emotional well-being.

ZARABANDA

The Nkisi Spirit, Zarabanda is the guardian of war, work, strength and destruction. Zarabanda can also be invoked and summoned in spells and rituals of witchcraft for either good or bad.

BRAZO FUERTE

The Nkisi Spirit, Brazo Fuerte is the guardian of earthquakes, volcanoes and natural disasters originating from within and inside the Earth. Brazo Fuerte can also be invoked and summoned to bring peace between individuals who are fighting that has been caused by disagreements.

NSAMBA NTALA

The Nkisi Spirit, Nsamba Ntala is the guardian of kaos and destruction.

INITIATIONS IN A TRADITIONAL CONGO MUNANZO

All of the following ceremonies are important initiations that an individual will undergo if they are considering becoming a part of a formal Congo religious temple. A Congo religious temple is called in Spanish "Munanzo". A Munanzo is a place of worship and where initiated individuals come together as a "family unit" to venerate the vast pantheon of Congo Spiritual Deities. A Munanzo is a place where your journey to the mystical supernatural world of the Congo Spirits begins. A Munanzo is a place of religious learning and also a place where magic begins and ends. If you are seeking initiation into the Congo religious Mysteries there are two things that you should know right now and be prepared for before beginning your spiritual journey.

The first is that it requires a lot of time and personal dedication. When you become initiated it will require much of your time to be spent at your Congo Munanzo working with your Godfather if you want to learn. That means a lot of time away from your home, time away from your personal relationships and time away from having fun. To complete the various steps and levels of Congo initiations could take many years.

The second thing is that it will require money for your religious education. Remember, this religion can really only be learned and experienced by direct initiation and participation. Each level of initiation requires that the individual give a donation fee (*Derecho*) to the Congo Temple. The *Derecho* is used to maintain the Congo Temple and to purchase the required ritual offerings which many times are expensive for the spirits. The reason that the initiation ceremonies are often times expensive is because of the complicity of each sacred ritual. As an experienced Tata of the Congo religion for many years, I can honestly tell you that I have seen and heard some real "horror stories" and the cost to redo or repair something that wasn't done correct the first time may even cost you more money than what you paid for the first time. That is of course, if you can find someone who is willing to do it for you !!!. It is better to pay the real price to someone who really knows what they are doing and to get it done right the first time. There are many other minor initiations associated with a Congo Munanzo but the following are the most important for an individual to do. The Congo experience is a very beautiful thing and the spirits will reward you. Patience and personal sacrifice are key elements to successful learning at a traditional Congo Munanzo. - *GUARANTEED* -

EGGUN SPIRITS INITIATION CEREMONY

The "Eggun Spirits Initiation Ceremony" links the new initiate to the world of their Ancestors. Without the permission, blessings and assistance of our Ancestors we will never be able to realize all of the good things that life holds for us. By undergoing this initiation an individual establishes a relationship with the world of the Ancestors so they will be better able to assist the individual with all the good things in life and to be able to overcome all difficulties that an individual may be faced with. It is important that a new initiate undergo this initiation ceremony so that they do not lose their way on their journey in this life. Although the Eggun Spirits Initiation Ceremony is of great importance to an individual initiate, it is not always a major initiation of every traditional Congo Munanzo.

The traditional Congo Eggun Spirits Altar.

RAYADO INITIATION CEREMONY

The "Rayado Initiation Ceremony" links the new initiate to the World of the Congo Spirits so that they will be better able to assist one with advancing in a positive direction in life. There are two parts of the Rayado Initiation Ceremony. The first "Rayado Initiation Ceremony" establishes a spiritual relationship between the Congo Spirits and the new initiate. The second "Rayado Initiation Ceremony," which is traditionally done 21 days after the first Rayado Initiation Ceremony gives the individual the ability to communicate and have command over the powerful Congo Deities. Both Rayado Initiation Ceremonies give an individual great protection against all harmful energy that may be affecting the individual or that may come their way. The Rayado Initiation Ceremony gives the individual the ability to leap over all obstacles of this life and will even protect an individual from untimely death. The Rayado Initiation Ceremony will make an individual invisible to any and all legal problems. This ceremony opens the third eye of the individual. It is only after doing these very important initiation ceremonies that an individual is fully accepted into the traditional Congo Munanzo Temple as a full-fledged member. The Rayado Initiation Ceremony can save your life.

THE CONGO SPIRIT LUCERO INITIATION CEREMONY

The "Congo Spirit Lucero Initiation Ceremony" is one of the major Congo rituals in which the new initiate will receive the mysteries of the actual "Nkisi" spirit to work with. The Congo Spirit Lucero is the Divine Gate Keeper and without his assistance and permission all forms of spiritual communication would be closed to the world of the Congo Spirits.

NGANGA INITIATION CEREMONY

The "Nganga Initiation Ceremony" is one of the most important of all of the initiation ceremonies associated with a traditional Congo Munanzo. When an individual undergoes this initiation, they receive the actual spirit

Mysteries of a particular Congo Spirit Deity to work with. The Mysteries of the Congo Spirits are usually received inside of an iron cauldron or ceramic pot that contains human bones along with many other magical ingredients and items to work with the Congo Spirit effectively in the supernatural magical realm. The cost will depend upon on which Congo Spirit Mysteries that the individual will be receiving.

MBELE INITAITION CEREMONY

The "Mbele Initiation Ceremony" is a ritual which gives the new initiate the religious right to be able to sacrifice four legged animals to the Congo Spirits. This initiation ceremony also gives the initiate the right to be able to perform the Rayado initiation on other individuals desiring to enter into the Congo Mysteries.

LA BAKUNFULA INITIATION CEREMONY

The initiation ceremony known as "*La Bakunfula*" can only be received by men. This initiation ceremony can only be received by one chosen individual of the Congo Munanzo who is the "right hand" of the presiding Tata of the Congo Munanzo. The official title of the "*Bakunfula*" is the "Sergeant at Arms". The *Bakunfula* is responsible for maintaining internal order at the Congo Munanzo. The *Bakunfula* along with the Tata is responsible for making sure that all of the sacred rituals and ceremonies of a Congo Munanzo are done and followed correctly by all of its members. The *Bakunfula* is also the individual who administers punishments for religious laws (Regla De Congo) violated by its members. Although this ceremony can be received by various male members, only one can officially be known as the "*Bakunfula*". The *Bakunfula* is also referred to as the "Mayordomo" by Caribbean Congo religious initiates.

TATA NIKISI MALONGO INITIATION CEREMONY

The last and final initiation that an individual can receive in a traditional Congo Munanzo is the "*Tata Nkisi Malongo Initiation Ceremony*". This initiation can only be received by men or by women who are no longer menstruating. When an individual receives this initiation and receives the spiritual Mysteries of *Tata Nkisi Malongo* they become one with the spiritual world and can command the powerful Congo Spirits as well as all of the spirits found in nature for whatever they want and however they want. This ceremony gives the individual great supernatural knowledge and occult powers to be able to even achieve invisibility and even shape shifting abilities. An individual must complete this very important initiation ceremony if they want to venture outside of their Congo Munanzo to one day start their own Congo Munanzo. When a woman receives this initiation they are referred to as *Yaya Nkisi Malongo*.

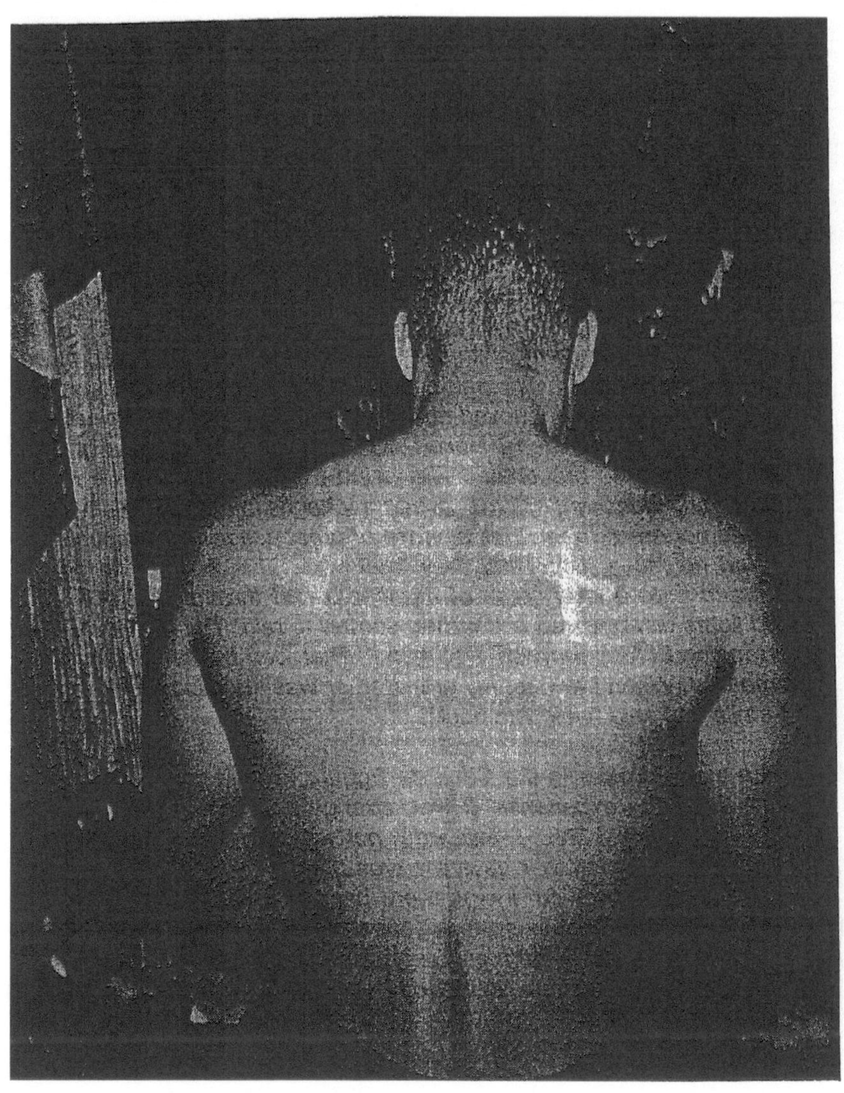

A new initiate receiving their first Afro-Caribbean Congo Rayado Initiation Ceremony.

THE BOVEDA ESPIRITUAL (SPIRITUAL BOVEDA)

The "*Boveda Espiritual*" refers to a spiritual altar that you should have set up in your temple or spiritual ritual area at all times. The Boveda Espiritual links the individual to the world of their personal Spiritual Guides. By linking to this world, the Spirit Guides will be better able to assist you and to bring you messages from their World to our World. The Boveda Espiritual altar is also a spiritual filter which collects harmful elements and bad vibration that may enter into your home. If your Boveda Espiritual altar is maintained correctly, your life should be spiritual clean and with little or no problems. The Boveda Espiritual is a place where you can go to salute and to communicate with your Spirit Guides on a daily basis. Spirit Guides are spirits that accompany you in this life. Spirit Guides can be ancestors or acquired spirit guides. The Boveda Espiritual consists of 7 or 9 glasses of water, a crucifix, flowers and a book of spiritual prayers that you can read directly in front of your Boveda Espiritual when you are praying alone or with a group prayer meeting called a "Misa Espiritual" or Spiritual Mass. The Boveda Espiritual should be set up on top of a small table covered with a white altar cloth. There should always be at least one white candle burning on it at all times. The water in the glasses should be disposed of and changed weekly. It is by meditating daily at your Boveda Espiritual altar that your abilities as a "Spiritual Medium" can be developed.

The Boveda Espiritual.

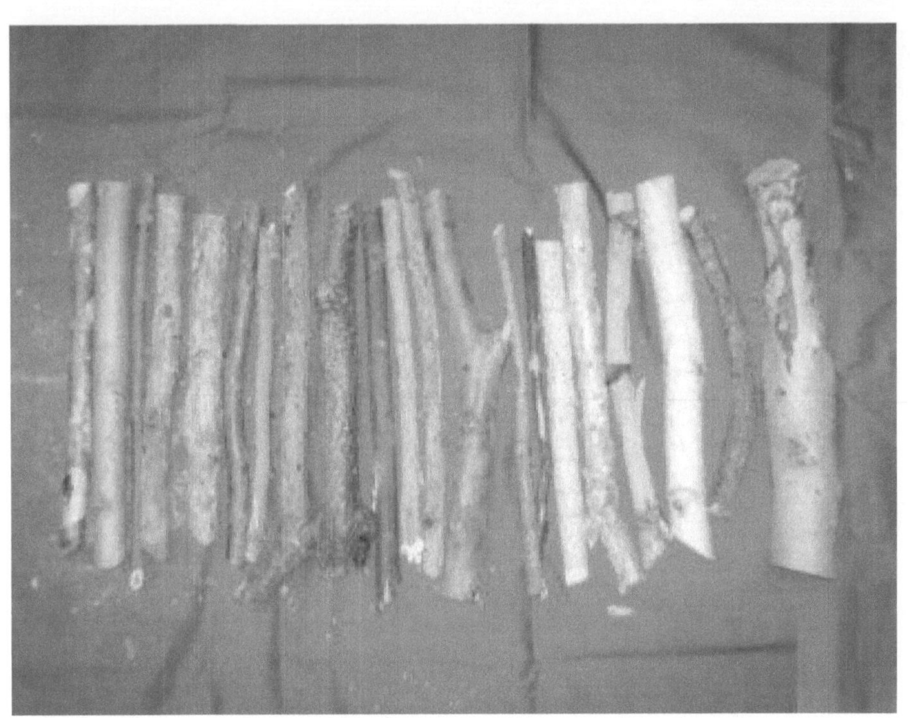

THE 21 PALOS

All of the Congo Spirit Ngangas contain a variety of natural magical ingredients that together empower the Congo Spirits so that they can manifest here on Earth and take on a variety of spiritual forms. In the Congolese religious tradition, these natural herbs are collectively called "*Nfinda*". It is believed that each of these herbs contains a specific type of magical ability and is inhabited by a spirit. Every traditional Congo Nganga must have a minimum of at least 21 Palos. These Palos can be made into powder or placed whole into the powerful Congo Spirit Nganga. These Palos reinforce the power of the Congo Spirits to be able to make magic begin or to end. Although the following list of 21 Palos seems to be the most common of these powerful Palos, a Congo Priest can pick and choose from a large variety of different types of magical Palos depending on the particular or specific type of Congo Spirit Nganga that they are preparing. The following list of 21 Palos can be used to prepare a "*Spiritual Nganga*" also known by initiates of Afro-Caribbean Congo religion as the "*Caldero Espiritual*".

1. ***PALO PARA MI*** - This palo is used to attract prosperity and love.

2. ***PALO YAMAO*** - This palo is used for both good and evil.

3. ***PALO BRONCO*** - This palo is used as a protection against witchcraft.

4. ***PALO CAJA*** - This palo is used to defeat an occult enemy.

5. ***PALO CHANGO*** - This palo is used to overcome all obstacles.

6. ***PALO VIRA MUNDO*** - This palo is used for both good to evil.

7. ***PALO TENGUE*** - This palo is used for spiritual protection.

8. ***PALO YAYA*** - This palo is used to reverse black magic back to the sender.

9. ***PALO VITITI CONGO*** - This palo is used to destroy your enemies.

10. ***PALO MORURU*** - This palo is used to close the roads of your enemies.

11. ***PALO CENIZA*** - This palo is used to maintain the energy of the Nganga.

12. ***PALO ROMPE HUESO*** - This palo is used to remove obstacles in your path.

13. ***PALO MONTE*** - This palo is used to invoke the power of the Congo Spirits.

14. ***PALO VARIA*** - This palo is used to dominate any individual or situation.

15. ***PALO MATA NEGRO*** - This palo is used to destroy black magic.

16. ***PALO CAMBIA RUMBO*** - This palo is used to destroy any individual.

17. ***PALO GUASIMA*** - This palo is used to control individuals.

18. ***PALO CIGUARRAYA*** - This palo is used to remove witchcraft.

19. ***PALO MAJAGUA*** - This palo is used to give the spirits super-natural power.

20. ***PALO VENCE BATALLA*** - This palo is used to win any spiritual battle or war.

21. ***PALO AMANSA GUAPO*** - This palo is used to attract money and love.

A picture of the sacred "Ceiba Spirit Tree". The Ceiba Tree is believed to be a gathering place of the Aje Spirits, the Eggun Spirits and the Congo Spirits. This powerful magical tree is the most important magical plants of the Afro-Caribbean Congo religious tradition. The Congo Spirits can be invoked and summoned directly in front of this sacred tree of the Congo religion.

SPIRITUAL NGANGA

(Caldero Espiritual)

A Spiritual Cauldron is an Nganga which does not contain any kind of human bone. This particular kind of Nganga is usually presented to individual who has not been formally initiated in the traditional Congo Rayado Ceremony. A Spiritual Cauldron is used to invoke an individual's Eggun Spirits, Spirit Guides or their personal Guardian Angel Spirits. An individual should not use this particular type of Nganga to perform spiritual cleanings or spiritual work for other individuals other than for themselves. Although traditionally this type of Nganga is usually prepared by an experienced Tata, it can be prepared by any individual who believes that their guardian spirits are requesting you to do so. The Ngangas of the traditional Congo Spirits must only be prepared and presented to you by an experienced initiated Tata Priest. If you have not received your basic initiation of the Congo religion then you will have to substitute red wine for the blood of the required animals.

Items Necessary for Spiritual Nganga

Large iron cauldron
One large smooth black stone (Matari)
Twenty-one quartz crystals
Twenty-one coins from various countries
Dirt from twenty-one different locations
One gold coin
One silver coin
Three round coconut shells (Chamalongo)
One quart Holy Water from 7 churches
White wine
Red wine
River water
Ocean water
Twenty-one palos
Twenty-one fresh herbs sacred to the Orixa Eleggua

Twenty-one palos in powdered form
twenty-one grains of paradise
Ache De Santo (powdered)
¼ pound of Mercury
¼ pound of precipitado rojo (Iron Oxidate powder)
Cigar
Rum
Bee's honey
Two 7 day white candles
One Life Size Plastic Human Skull

Live animals needed

Two black roosters

Preparation of Spiritual Nganga

1. In a large bowl, prepare an omiero using the twenty-one herbs sacred to the Orixa Eleggua. Use the twenty-one grains of paradise, ocean water, river water and the milk from the coconuts. After you have prepared the omiero, place the stone and the twenty-one quartz crystals into the omiero liquid and allow them to soak for a 24 hour period. Light a large 7 day candle next to the bowl. This procedure should be done outside.

2. After the 24 hours, wash the iron cauldron with some omiero.

3. Take a mouthful of rum and spray directly into the caldron.

4. Light a cigar and blow the smoke directly into the cauldron.

5. After you have completed this procedure the vessel which will be housing the spirit has been baptized and is now ready

to receive the other items. Pour the mercury into the bottom of the iron cauldron.

6. In a large bucket, mix all of the dirt's, powdered palos, Ache De Santo and the precipitado rojo together. Mix well.

7. After you have mixed all of the dirt's together, pour in some of the prepared omiero mixture into the bucket containing the dirt and make a thick paste mixture.

8. Using the paste dirt mixture place a one inch layer over the bottom of the iron cauldron.

9. On top of this mixture, place the stone and the twenty-one quartz crystals positioned around the stone in a complete circle.

10. After you have done that, place another layer of dirt on top of those items.

11. Place all of the coins on this layer.

12. Place another layer of dirt.

13. Place all of the remaining dirt paste on top of these items so the dirt comes all the way to the top of the cauldron.

14. Hammer all of the palos in a circle into the circle around the edges of the iron caldron.

15. Place the prepared Lungowa (a hooked stick), the Mpaka and the Cana Brava into the cauldron.

16. After you have fully mounted the spiritual Nganga, recite the initiation prayers and mambos (songs) that are provided in this book.

17. After the mambos, the entire Nganga should be placed and buried into a large hole at the base of a Ceiba tree or other large tree. The Nganga should be fed the blood of a black rooster and then buried for a total of 21 days.

18. After the 21 days, uncover the Nganga and feed it again the blood of a black rooster.

19. After you have feed the Nganga, pour bee's honey, red wine, white wine and blow cigar smoke over the Nganga.

20. After feeding check to see if the offerings were accepted by the spirit by using the four coconut shell pieces for divination.

21. If the spirit responds favorably, then a series of mambos should be sung to the spirit. After this, the spirit can be safely placed into its final resting place along with a white candle.

The Nganga of the Congo Spirit Zarabanda.

HOW TO PREPARE THE MPAKA

The Mpaka is perhaps one of the most important keys to the Nganga. The mpaka in itself is a miniature nganga which can be transported easily. The mpaka holds the complete mysteries of the spirit. The mpaka contains the spiritual DNA of that particular spirit and using the Mpaka, the Palero Priest can duplicate and give birth to another spirit of the same type without the mysteries contained and found in the nganga of the large cast iron cauldron. A Mayombero can take his Mpaka anywhere in the world and by using the mysteries contained within it rebuild his nganga. The Mpaka is the third eye and the ear of the spirit. When a glass mirror is placed on the open end of the Mpaka to cover the magical ingredients, it is termed "*Vititi Mensu*" meaning the "all seeing eye". With the Mpaka, a Mayombero priest can duplicate an unlimited amount of prepared ngangas of the same exact spirit.

<u>Items Necessary</u>

1. *One large bull's horn (unfinished)*
2. *One medium lightning stone (Matari)*
3. *One tablespoon liquid mercury*
4. *Dirt from various locations*
5. *Three Quartz Crystals*
6. *Twenty-one coins from around the World*
7. *Powdered Bats*
8. *Powdered Snakes*
9. *Powdered Spiders*
10. *Powdered Chameleon Lizard*
11. *Twenty-one powdered palos*
12. *Deer horn powder*
13. *Tooth from a wolf*
14. *Tooth from a tiger*
15. *Tooth from a coyote*
16. *Tongue and eyes from a rooster*
17. *Tongue and eyes from a rooster Guinea Hen*

18. Tongue and eyes from a Parrot
19. Bones from a vulture
20. Iron Oxidate Powder
21. Twenty-one powdered herbs
22. Fresh herbs for an omiero
23. Fingernail cuttings, toe nail cuttings and body hair from various parts of the body of the owner of the spiritual nganga.
24. One round mirror (The mirror must fit perfectly into the open end of the Bull's horn)
25. Fast dry cement

*** DEPENDING ON THE PARTICULAR SPIRIT NGANGA THAT YOU ARE PREPARING, THE NUMBER OF FRESH HERBS USED IN THE PREPARATION OF THE OMIERO WILL VARY. FOR EXAMPLE: IF YOU ARE PREPARING A MPAKA FOR THE SPIRIT ZARABANDA, YOU WILL USE 9 HERBS SACRED TO THE SPIRIT ZARABANDA OR SACRED TO THE ORIXA OGGUN - ALL OF THESE FRESH HERBS ARE AVAILABLE FROM ANY WELL STOCKED BOTANICA ***

Live animals needed

Two black roosters

Preparation of the Mpaka

1. In a large mixing bowl, prepare an omiero using the fresh herbs. Use the grains of paradise, ocean water, river water, May rain water and the milk from one coconut in the preparation of the omiero. After you have prepared the omiero, place the lightening stone, the three quartz crystals, the 21 coins and the bull's horn into the omiero mixture to soak and remain for 24 hours. Light a large seven day white religious glass candle and set it next to the bowl of omiero to give light and blessing to the items that will go into the mpaka.

2. After the 24 hours, remove the bull's horn.

3. Take a mouthful of rum and spray it directly into the empty bull's horn.

4. light a cigar and blow it directly into the bull's horn.

5. After you have finished this procedure, the bull's horn which will be housing the magical elements of the spirit has been baptized and is now ready to receive the other sacred items.

6. Pour the mercury into the bottom of the empty bull's horn.

7. In a large bucket, mix all of the dirts, powdered herbs and palos, the iron oxidate powder, the powdered spiders, the powdered bats, the powdered snakes, the powdered chameleons, the powdered spiders, the deer horn powder and the hair and nail clippings together, mixing well.

8. After you have mixed all of these magical ingredients together, pour in some of the omiero mixture into the bucket containing the magical mixture of ingredients and make a thick past like mixture.

9. Add a small amount of the past mixture into the empty bull's horn and firmly pack it down.

10. Place the lightening stone into the bull's horn.

11. Add some more of the paste mixture into the bull's horn.

12. Place the quartz crystals into the bull's horn and cover with the paste mixture.

13. Place all of the coins into the bull's horn and cover with the paste mixture.

14. Place the wolf's tooth, the tiger tooth, the human teeth, the vulture bones, the tongues from the rooster, parrot and the guinea hen into the horn and then cover these items with the remaining paste mixture. Firmly pack all of these ingredients into the bull's horn. (Place the red cloth bundle containing your personal items into the horn)

15. Feed the mpaka the blood from one rooster and allow it to remain for 3 hours.

16. After the 3 hours, light a white candle and allow the wax to drip over the top of the bull's horn and to completely cover the open end of it.

17. Place the mirror onto the top of the bull's horn on top of the wax.

18. After the wax has dried with the mirror embedded in it, seal the mirror onto the bull's horn with the fast dry cement with a good area of the mirror showing.

19. After the cement has dried, feed the spirit mpaka again with the blood of the other rooster.

THE OUTSIDE OF THE MPAKA CAN BE DECORATED WITH STRANDS OF BEADS AND COWRIE SHELLS. THE COLORS OR PATTERN OF THE BEADS WILL DEPEND ON WHICH SPIRIT THE MPAKA IS BEING MADE FOR. THE COLORS FOR THE CONGO SPIRITUAL NGANGA ARE MULTI-COLORED BEADS.

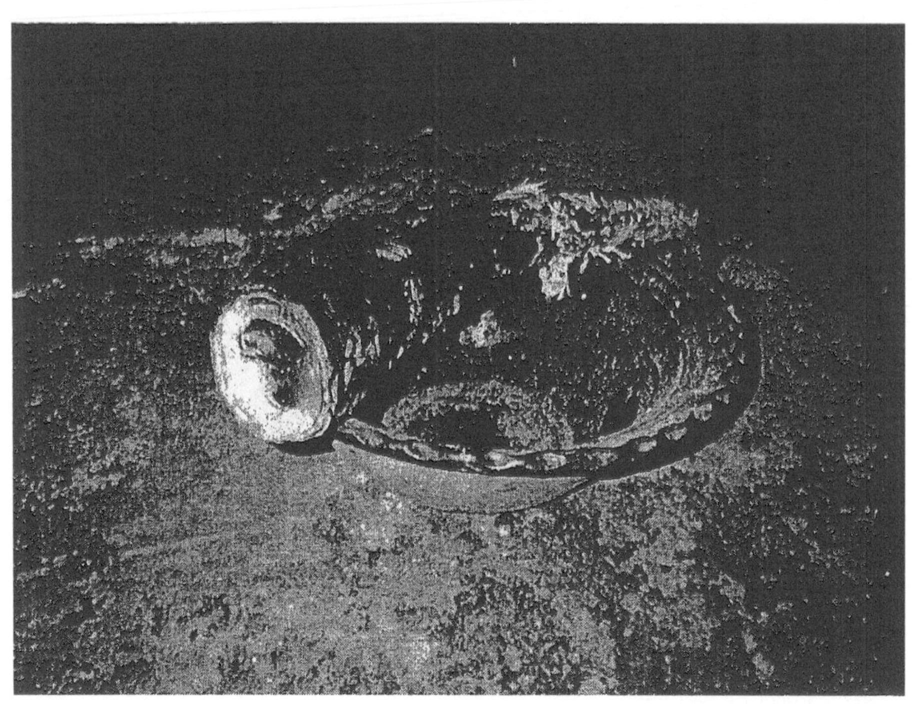

A traditional Mpaka of the Congo Spirits.

HOW TO PREPARE THE OZUN OF THE NGANGA

The Ozun of the Nganga (Ozun De Muerto) is another important element of the spirit Nganga. The Ozun of the Nganga is the spiritual antenna of the spirit nganga. The Ozun of the Nganga allows the spirit to receive clear messages and vibration to assist the Mayombero with their spiritual requests and spells.

<u>Items Necessary</u>

1. *One standing metal trident (pitchfork)*
2. *One medium size clay bowl*
3. *Dirt from various locations*
4. *Twenty-one powdered palos*
5. *One tablespoon of liquid Mercury*
6. *Twenty-one herbs sacred to the Orixa Elegua*
7. *Deer horn powder*
8. *Ache De Santo herb (powdered)*
9. *Twenty-one coins*
10. *One metal key*
11. *Coconut water*
12. *Holy water*
13. *River water*
14. *Ocean water*
15. *Bee's honey*
16. *Fast dry cement*
17. *Twenty-one Cowrie shells*

<u>Live animals needed</u>

One black rooster
One Guinea hen

Preparation of the Mpaka

1. In a large mixing bowl, prepare an omiero using the twenty-one herbs, the 21 grains of paradise, ocean water, river water, holy water and the coconut water in the preparation of the omiero. After you have prepared the omiero, place the metal trident (OZUN), all of the coins and the key into the omiero liquid mixture. Light a white candle next to the bowl and allow the items to remain for a 24 hour period of time.

2. Take a mouthful of rum and spray it into the clay bowl.

3. Light a cigar and blow the smoke into the clay dish.

4. In a large bucket, mix all of the dirts together with the 21 powdered palos, the human bone powder, the deer horn powder and the Ache De Santo. MIX WELL.

5. After you have mixed all of the items together, pour in some of the omiero mixture into the bucket containing the dirt mixture and make a thick past mixture.

6. Place the standing trident into the center of the clay bowl.

7. Place the dirt mixture into the clay dish completely around the base of the trident.

8. Firmly pack down the dirt mixture

9. Place the key on top of the dirt mixture.

10. Place the 21 coins on top of the dirt mixture.

11. Pour the mercury on top of the dirt mixture.

12. Mix the fast dry cement with the liquid from the omiero.

13. Pour the cement on top of the dirt, the other magical items and around the base of the trident.

14. Decorate the top of the flat cement surface with the 21 cowrie shells by forming a complete circle around the inner edge of the clay dish.

15. After the cement has dried, feed the Ozun of the Nganga with the blood of a rooster and a guinea hen.

16. After the Ozun of the Nganga is finished, set it next to the Spirit Nganga along with a white candle.

FEED THE OZUN OF THE NGANGA EVERY TIME YOU FEED THE SPIRITUAL NGANGA AND THE SPIRITUAL LUCERO.

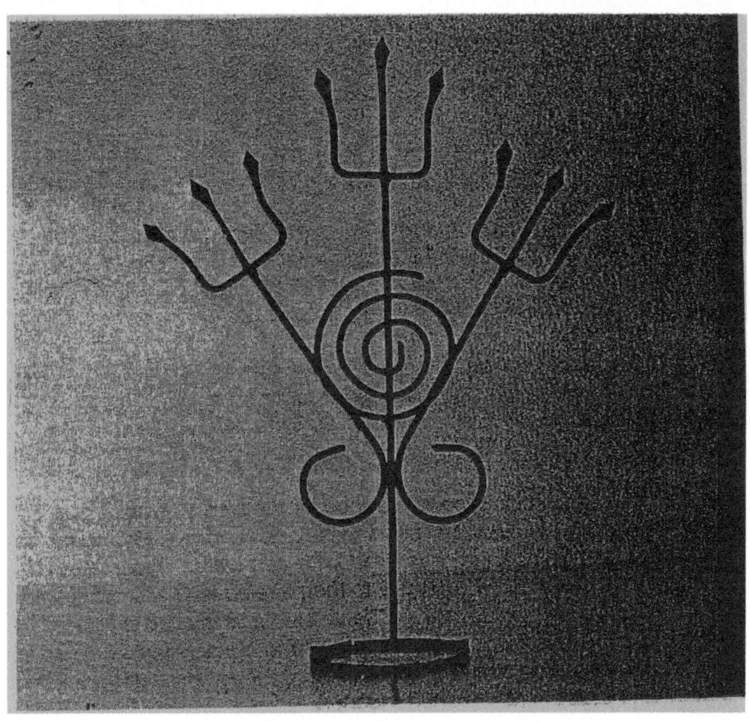

A TRADITIONAL OZUN DE MUERTO BEFORE BEING PREPARED.

HOW TO PREPARE THE CANA BRAVA

The Cana Brava is another magical element to the successful manifestation of the spirit of the nganga. Cana Brava is a specific type of bamboo used by Mayomberos in the preparation of their ngangas. The Cana Brava which is naturally hollow is filled with a variety of items and liquids. The items and liquids are then sealed inside of the Cana Brava and placed in an upright position in the nganga. The Cana Brava is known as the thermometer of the spirit. The Cana Brava is an important part and element of the completed nganga because it is used to keep the energy of the spirit balanced and its temperature cool.

Items Necessary

1. *One piece of hollow Bamboo (12 -24 inches in length)*
2. *One tablespoon of sand from the Ocean*
3. *One tablespoon of sand from the River*
4. *River water*
5. *Ocean water*
6. *May Rain Water*
7. *One tablespoon of liquid Mercury*
8. *Fast Dry Cement*
9. *Virgin wax (White)*

Preparation of the Cana Brava

1. Seal one of the open ends of the hollow Cana Brava with fast dry cement and virgin wax. 2. The amount of cement and wax poured into the hollow Cana Brava should be about 2 inches. 3. After the cement and wax have dried and have hardened, wash the Cana Brava in River Water. 4. After you have washed the Cana Brava, add the sand from the ocean and the river into the hollow Cana Brava. 5. Pour the mercury into the hollow Cana Brava. 6. Pour an even amount of May Rain Water, River Water and the Ocean Water into the hollow Cana Brava. 7. The amount of

combined waters should come up to the level about 2 inches from the opening. 8. Pour in about 1 inch of virgin wax into the Cana Brava to cover the liquids and to seal them into the Cana Brava. 9. After the wax has completely dried, pour in fast dry cement into the remaining hollow end of the Cana Brava. 10. Allow it to dry for 3 hours. After the 3 hours, place the Cana Brava into the spirit nganga in a standing upwards position.

THE CANA BRAVA SHOULD BE CHECKED AT LEAST ONCE A WEEK TO MAKE SURE THAT THE WATERS INSIDE HAVE NOT EVAPORATED. IF YOU ARE WORKING A LOT WITH YOUR SPIRIT NGANGA, IT IS COMMON FOR THE HEAT AND ENEGRY OF THE SPIRIT TO EVAPORATE THE LIQUIDS. IF THIS OCCURS, SIMPLY OPEN THE CANA BRAVA UP AND REPLACE THE EVAPORATED LIQUIDS AND SEAL IT UP AGAIN. IF YOUR CANA BRAVA EXPLOADS OR CRACKS AND THE LIQUID LEAKS OUT, THEN THIS IS A SURE SIGN THAT SOMEONE HAS SPIRITUALLY ATTACKED YOU AND YOU BETTER REACT FAST AND QUICK TO REVERSE IT BACK TO THEM IN A HURRY. ALL OF THE INITIATED CONGO PRIESTS OUT THERE WHO HAVE AN AUTHENTIC CONGO NGANGA KNOWN WHAT I AM TALIKING ABOUT. (SPIRITUAL WAR)

A picture of the bamboo tree before used as the Cana Brava.

HOW TO PREPARE THE KIYUMBA (SKULL)

The Kiyumba is the term that refers to the human skull that must be present in the nganga. Because the human skulls that are used in the preparing of traditional Congo spirit ngangas are usually purchased from biological supply houses are empty, meaning they do not have a brain, it is necessary to prepare an artificial spirit brain to be placed on the inside of the brain cavity of the hollow skull. By preparing the kiyumba you will be able to program your spirit to focus and concentrate on a specific or numerous tasks at hand. The Spiritual Cauldron does not contain any human bone in its preparation. When preparing a Spiritual cauldron you should use a cement or plastic human skull to spiritually represent the spirit that lives in the nganga.

Items Necessary

1. Dirt from 21 different locations
2. Dirt from the four corners from outside your house
3. Twenty-one powdered palos
4. Ache De Santo herb (powdered)
5. River water
6. May rain water
7. Holy water
8. Ocean water
9. Three pieces of gold
10. Three pieces of silver
11. Twenty-one coins from around the World
12. Coconut milk
13. One used key
14. One tablespoon of liquid Mercury
15. One tablespoon of Iron Oxidate powder
16. One Lightning stone
17. Two Magnetic stones
18. Powdered Ceiba Tree
19. One Quartz Crystal
20. One roll of 100% Cotton

21. Twenty-one fresh herbs of Orixa Elegua
22. Honey
23. Red wine

Live animals needed

One black rooster

Preparation of the Kiyumba

1. Mix all of the dirts, the iron oxidate powder, the powdered palos and the powdered ceiba leafs together in a large mixing bowl.

2. Add the coconut milk and the waters to the mixture making a thick paste.

3. Insert the paste and all of the other remaining items into the skull through the bottom or the top and completely fill it up.

4. After it has been filled cover the hole with the cotton.

5. After the cotton is inserted firmly, pour melted candle wax into the hole to seal up all of the ingredients.

6. Soak the skull in an omiero mixture made from the 21 fresh herbs.

7. Set the skull into a large bowl and then pour the omiero over the top of it along with the honey and red wine.

8. Feed the skull with the blood of a black rooster and then light a white candle and sit it next to the skull.

9. Allow the skull to soak for at least 24 hours before placing it into the spirit nganga.

HOW TO PREPARE A LUCERO FOR THE SPIRITUAL CAULDRON

1. In a large bowl, prepare an omiero using the twenty-one herbs sacred to the Orixa Eleggua. Use the 21 grains of paradise, ocean water, river water, May rain water and the milk from the coconut in the preparation of the omiero. After you have prepared the omiero, place the stone from the mountain into the omiero liquid. 2. Recite the general Congo prayer to the Spirit Lucero and sacrifice a rooster. Allow the blood to spill over the stone. 3. Pour bee's honey over the stone and blow cigar smoke and rum over the stone. 4. Allow to soak for a 24 hour period. 5. Light a large, seven day, white candle next to the bowl. 6. Paint the symbol of Lucero Vira Mundo on the inside bottom of the clay bowl and seal the design with melted virgin wax. 7. Take a mouthful of rum and spray it directly into the clay bowl. 8. Light a cigar and blow the smoke directly into the clay bowl. 9. In a separate large bucket, mix all of the dirt's, powdered palos, powdered fighting cock's spur bone powder, iron oxidate powder and the fast dry cement together. Mix well. 10. After you have mixed all of these ingredients, pour in some of the prepared omiero mixture into the bucket containing the dirt and make a thick paste like mixture.11. Place the gold, the silver, the peonia seeds, the key and the coin into the clay bowl. 12. Using the paste like mixture, place a one inch layer over the items and the design in the clay bowl.13. On top of this mixture, place the stone from the mountain. 14. Using the cement paste, completely cover the stone until it you have shaped it into a face. 15. Place the shells for the eyes and a mouth. Before place the shell for the mouth, make a small hole and place the parrot tongue, the guinea hens tongue and the tongue from the rooster. Place the shell over these items. 16. Place the three feathers into the top of the head. 17. Allow it to dry. 18. After it has dried, bury and place Lucero at a crossroads for 21 days and nights.

19. After the 21 days have passed, the Lucero can be unearthed and fed the following animals in this order, Rooster and the Guinea Hen. 20. After you have fed Lucero, Pour bee's honey and blow cigar smoke and rum (chamba) over him. 21. The sacrificed animals should be buried in the same hole along with 21cents. 22. After the feeding check to see of the offerings were accepted by the spirit by using the four coconut shell pieces (Chamalongo) for divination. 23. If the spirit is satisfied and responds favorably, then a series of mambos should be sung to bring the spirit closer to you. 24. The spirit Lucero should be placed and kept with the corresponding Nganga.

The spiritual signature of the Congo Spirit, Lucero Vira Mundo.

A GENERAL INVOCATION PRAYER TO THE CONGO SPIRITS

The following is a general invocation prayer to the Congo Spirits that can be used when you are preparing your Spiritual Cauldron. This general prayer can also be used at any time that you would like to summon the spirits or to simply give thanks and praise to your spirit guides. This general prayer can be recited while standing directly in front of your Spiritual Cauldron.

1. While standing directly in front of your Spiritual Cauldron bend down and cross your hands and arms and tap the ground three times and recite the following: *Salamalekun, Malekunsala.*

2. After reciting this opening sacred prayer phrase then stand back up and while facing directly in front of the Spiritual Nganga recite the following invocation prayer;

CON LA LICENCIA DE NZAMBI.
(With the blessing and permission of Nzambi, the God of the Heavens and the Earth).

SALA MALEKUN, MALEKUN SALA.
(I give you thanks and praise).

CON LA BENDICION DE LOS BRUJOS CONGOS ANTEPASADOS, MIS ANCESTROS Y MIS GUIAS ESPIRITUALES QUE ESTAN A LOS PIES DE NZAMBI.

(With the permission and the blessings of the Congo Priests who have died and are kneeling at the feet of Nzambi in light). (With the permission and the blessings of my ancestors who have died and are kneeling at the feet of Nzambi in light). (With the permission and the blessings of my spirit guides who walk with me and protect me with light).

SALA MALEKUN, MALEKUN SALA.
(I give you thanks and praise).

CON LA LICENCIA DE LUCERO,
(With the blessings and permission of the Congo Spirit Lucero).

SALA MALEKUN, MALEKUN SALA.
(I give you thanks and praise).

CON LA LICENCIA DE KOBAYENDE
(With the blessings and permission of the Congo Spirit Kobayende).

SALA MALEKUN, MALEKUN SALA.
(I give you thanks and praise).

CON LA LICENCIA DE CENTELLA NDOKI
(With the blessings and permission of the Congo Spirit Centella Ndoki).

SALA MALEKUN, MALEKUN SALA.
(I give you thanks and praise).

CON LA LICENCIA DE GURUNFINDA
(With the blessings and permission of the Congo Spirit Gurunfinda).

SALA MALEKUN, MALEKUN SALA.
(I give you thanks and praise).

CON LA LICENCIA DE MADRE DE AGUA
(With the blessings and permission of the Congo Spirit Madre De Agua).

SALA MALEKUN, MALEKUN SALA.
(I give you thanks and praise).

CON LA LICENCIA DE CALUNGA
(With the blessings and permission of the Congo Spirit Calunga).

SALA MALEKUN, MALEKUN SALA.
(I give you thanks and praise).

CON LA LICENCIA DE MAMA SHOLAN
(With the blessings and permission of the Congo Spirit Mama Sholan).

SALA MALEKUN, MALEKUN SALA.
(I give you thanks and praise).

CON LA LICENCIA DE TIEMPO VIEJO
(With the blessings and permission of the Congo Spirit Tiempo Viejo).

SALA MALEKUN, MALEKUN SALA.
(I give you thanks and praise).

CON LA LICENCIA DE CABO RONDO
(With the blessings and permission of the Congo Spirit Cabo Rondo).

SALA MALEKUN, MALEKUN SALA.
(I give you thanks and praise).

CON LA LICENCIA DE SIETE RAYOS
(With the blessings and permission of the Congo Spirit Siete Rayos).

SALA MALEKUN, MALEKUN SALA.
(I give you thanks and praise).

CON LA LICENCIA DE TIEMBLA TIERRA
(With the blessings and permission of the Congo Spirit Tiembla Tierra).

SALA MALEKUN, MALEKUN SALA.
(I give you thanks and praise).

CON LA LICENCIA DE ZARABANDA
(With the blessings and permission of the Congo Spirit Zarabanda).

SALA MALEKUN, MALEKUN SALA.
(I give you thanks and praise).

CON LA LICENCIA DE BRAZO FUERTE
(With the blessings and permission of the Congo Spirit Brazo Fuerte).

SALA MALEKUN, MALEKUN SALA.
(I give you thanks and praise).

CON LA LICENCIA DE NSAMBA NTALA
(With the blessings and permission of the Congo Spirit Nsamba Ntala).

SALA MALEKUN, MALEKUN SALA.
(I give you thanks and praise).

LUCERO BRILLUMBI NDOKI INFIERNO VIRA MUNDO.
(Spirit Lucero, it is you who lights and turns the World).

KOBAYENDE BRILLUMBI NDOKI INFIERNO VIRA MUNDO.
(Spirit Kobayende, it is you who lights and turns the World).

CENTELLA NDOKI BRILLUMBI NDOKI INFIERNO VIRA MUNDO.
(Spirit Centella Ndoki, it is you who lights and turns the World).

GURUNFINDA BRILLUMBI NDOKI INFIERNO VIRA MUNDO.
(Spirit Gurunfina, it is you who lights and turns the World).

MADRE DE AGUA BRILLUMBI NDOKI INFIERNO VIRA MUNDO.
(Spirit Madre De Agua, it is you who lights and turns the World).

CALUNGA BRILLUMBI NDOKI INFIERNO VIRA MUNDO.
(Spirit Calunga, it is you who lights and turns the World).

MAMA SHOLAN BRILLUMBI NDOKI INFIERNO VIRA MUNDO.
(Spirit Mama Sholan, it is you who lights and turns the World).

TIEMPO VIEJO BRILLUMBI NDOKI INFIERNO VIRA MUNDO.
(Spirit Tiempo Viejo, it is you who lights and turns the World).

CABO RONDO BRILLUMBI NDOKI INFIERNO VIRA MUNDO.
(Spirit Cabo Rondo, it is you who lights and turns the World).

SIETE RAYOS BRILLUMBI NDOKI INFIERNO VIRA MUNDO.
(Spirit Siete Rayos, it is you who lights and turns the World).

TIEMBLA TIERRA BRILLUMBI NDOKI INFIERNO VIRA MUNDO.
(Spirit Tiembla Tierra, it is you who lights and turns the World).

ZARABANDA BRILLUMBI NDOKI INFIERNO VIRA MUNDO.
(Spirit Zarabanda, it is you who lights and turns the World).

BRAZO FUERTE BRILLUMBI NDOKI INFIERNO VIRA MUNDO.
(Spirit Brazo Fuerte, it is you who lights and turns the World).

NSAMBA NTALA BRILLUMBI NDOKI INFIERNO VIRA MUNDO.
(Spirit Nsamba Ntala, it is you who lights and turns the World).

WHO IS THE GREATEST IN HEAVEN*?* *NZAMBI*
WHO IS THE GREATEST IN HEAVEN*?* *NZAMBI*
WHO IS THE GREATEST IN HEAVEN*?* *NZAMBI*
WHO ARE YOU*?*
WHO ARE YOU*?*
WHO ARE YOU*?*

SAY YOUR SPIRITUAL REQUEST HERE

SPIRITUAL COMMUNICATION & INVOKING THE SPIRITS

THE FOLLOWING CONGO RITUAL IS HOW TO INVOKE AND SUMMON THE POWERFUL CONGO DIETIES FROM THEIR WORLD TO OUR WORLD. THIS CEREMONY CAN BE USED BY INITIATES FROM ANY CONGO RELIGIOUS TRADITION AS A POWERFUL PRAYER TO INCREASE THEIR SUPERNATURAL POWER, CONTROL AND SPIRITUAL INSIGHT. IT IS ONLY BY INVOKING THESE POWERUL CONGO ENTITIES AT REGULAR INTERVALS THAT YOUR RELATIONSHIP WITH THE CONGO SPIRITS CAN BE ESTABLISHED SO THAT YOU WILL BE ABLE TO BECOME ONE WITH THEM. THIS VERY IMPORTANT RITUAL SHOULD BE DONE AT LEAST (1) TIME A WEEK DIRECTLY AT 12 MIDNIGHT. AFTER YOU HAVE ESTABLISHED A RITUAL RELATIONSHIP WITH THE CONGO SPIRITS THERE IS NOTHING THAT WOULD BE IMPOSSIBLE TO MAGICALLY ACCOMPLISH WITH YOUR SPIRITS. THIS SACRED RITUAL SPIRITUALLY LINKS THE SPIRITS TO YOU SO THAT YOU WILL BE ABLE TO COMMAND THEM TO DO YOUR BIDDING.

Instructions

1. Draw a large circle using chalk or pemba (7 feet in diameter around the Spiritual Cauldron).

2. Inside the large circle draw the spirit signature of the Spiritual Cauldron within the sacred circle. The spirit signature should be as large as the circle.

3. Blow cigar smoke directly into the Spiritual Cauldron and directly on the Spiritual Lucero.

4. Using your mouth, spray rum directly on the Spiritual Cauldron and the Spiritual Lucero.

5. Light (3) white candles directly in front of the Spiritual Cauldron and the Spiritual Lucero.

6. While standing directly in front of your Spiritual Cauldron bend down and cross your hands and arms and tap the ground three times and recite the following: *Salamalekun, Malekunsala.*

7. After reciting this opening sacred prayer phrase then stand back up and while facing directly in front of the Spiritual Nganga recite the following invocation prayer;

CON LA LICENCIA DE NZAMBI.
(With the blessing and permission of Nzambi, the God of the Heavens and the Earth).

SALA MALEKUN, MALEKUN SALA.
(I give you thanks and praise).

CON LA BENDICION DE LOS BRUJOS CONGOS ANTEPASADOS, MIS ANCESTROS Y MIS GUIAS ESPIRITUALES QUE ESTAN A LOS PIES DE NZAMBI.

(With the permission and the blessings of the Congo Priests who have died and are kneeling at the feet of Nzambi in light). (With the permission and the blessings of my ancestors who have died and are kneeling at the feet of Nzambi in light). (With the permission and the blessings of my spirit guides who walk with me and protect me with light).

SALA MALEKUN, MALEKUN SALA.
(I give you thanks and praise).

CON LA LICENCIA DE LUCERO,
(With the blessings and permission of the Congo Spirit Lucero).

SALA MALEKUN, MALEKUN SALA.
(I give you thanks and praise).

CON LA LICENCIA DE KOBAYENDE
(With the blessings and permission of the Congo Spirit Kobayende).

SALA MALEKUN, MALEKUN SALA.
(I give you thanks and praise).

CON LA LICENCIA DE CENTELLA NDOKI
(With the blessings and permission of the Congo Spirit Centella Ndoki).

SALA MALEKUN, MALEKUN SALA.
(I give you thanks and praise).

CON LA LICENCIA DE GURUNFINDA
(With the blessings and permission of the Congo Spirit Gurunfinda).

SALA MALEKUN, MALEKUN SALA.
(I give you thanks and praise).

CON LA LICENCIA DE MADRE DE AGUA
(With the blessings and permission of the Congo Spirit Madre De Agua).

SALA MALEKUN, MALEKUN SALA.
(I give you thanks and praise).

CON LA LICENCIA DE CALUNGA
(With the blessings and permission of the Congo Spirit Calunga).

SALA MALEKUN, MALEKUN SALA.
(I give you thanks and praise).

CON LA LICENCIA DE MAMA SHOLAN
(With the blessings and permission of the Congo Spirit Mama Sholan).

SALA MALEKUN, MALEKUN SALA.
(I give you thanks and praise).

CON LA LICENCIA DE TIEMPO VIEJO
(With the blessings and permission of the Congo Spirit Tiempo Viejo).

SALA MALEKUN, MALEKUN SALA.
(I give you thanks and praise).

CON LA LICENCIA DE CABO RONDO
(With the blessings and permission of the Congo Spirit Cabo Rondo).

SALA MALEKUN, MALEKUN SALA.
(I give you thanks and praise).

CON LA LICENCIA DE SIETE RAYOS
(With the blessings and permission of the Congo Spirit Siete Rayos).

SALA MALEKUN, MALEKUN SALA.
(I give you thanks and praise).

CON LA LICENCIA DE TIEMBLA TIERRA
(With the blessings and permission of the Congo Spirit Tiembla Tierra).

SALA MALEKUN, MALEKUN SALA.
(I give you thanks and praise).

CON LA LICENCIA DE ZARABANDA
(With the blessings and permission of the Congo Spirit Zarabanda).

SALA MALEKUN, MALEKUN SALA.
(I give you thanks and praise).

CON LA LICENCIA DE BRAZO FUERTE
(With the blessings and permission of the Congo Spirit Brazo Fuerte).

SALA MALEKUN, MALEKUN SALA.
(I give you thanks and praise).

CON LA LICENCIA DE NSAMBA NTALA
(With the blessings and permission of the Congo Spirit Nsamba Ntala).

SALA MALEKUN, MALEKUN SALA.
(I give you thanks and praise).

LUCERO BRILLUMBI NDOKI INFIERNO VIRA MUNDO.
(Spirit Lucero, it is you who lights and turns the World).

KOBAYENDE BRILLUMBI NDOKI INFIERNO VIRA MUNDO.
(Spirit Kobayende, it is you who lights and turns the World).

CENTELLA NDOKI BRILLUMBI NDOKI INFIERNO VIRA MUNDO.
(Spirit Centella Ndoki, it is you who lights and turns the World).

GURUNFINDA BRILLUMBI NDOKI INFIERNO VIRA MUNDO.
(Spirit Gurunfina, it is you who lights and turns the World).

MADRE DE AGUA BRILLUMBI NDOKI INFIERNO VIRA MUNDO.
(Spirit Madre De Agua, it is you who lights and turns the World).

CALUNGA BRILLUMBI NDOKI INFIERNO VIRA MUNDO.
(Spirit Calunga, it is you who lights and turns the World).

MAMA SHOLAN BRILLUMBI NDOKI INFIERNO VIRA MUNDO.
(Spirit Mama Sholan, it is you who lights and turns the World).

TIEMPO VIEJO BRILLUMBI NDOKI INFIERNO VIRA MUNDO.
(Spirit Tiempo Viejo, it is you who lights and turns the World).

CABO RONDO BRILLUMBI NDOKI INFIERNO VIRA MUNDO.
(Spirit Cabo Rondo, it is you who lights and turns the World).

SIETE RAYOS BRILLUMBI NDOKI INFIERNO VIRA MUNDO.
(Spirit Siete Rayos, it is you who lights and turns the World).

TIEMBLA TIERRA BRILLUMBI NDOKI INFIERNO VIRA MUNDO.
(Spirit Tiembla Tierra, it is you who lights and turns the World).

ZARABANDA BRILLUMBI NDOKI INFIERNO VIRA MUNDO.
(Spirit Zarabanda, it is you who lights and turns the World).

BRAZO FUERTE BRILLUMBI NDOKI INFIERNO VIRA MUNDO.
(Spirit Brazo Fuerte, it is you who lights and turns the World).

NSAMBA NTALA BRILLUMBI NDOKI INFIERNO VIRA MUNDO.
(Spirit Nsamba Ntala, it is you who lights and turns the World).

WHO IS THE GREATEST IN HEAVEN? *NZAMBI*
WHO IS THE GREATEST IN HEAVEN? *NZAMBI*
WHO IS THE GREATEST IN HEAVEN? *NZAMBI*
WHO ARE YOU?
WHO ARE YOU?
WHO ARE YOU?

SALA MALEKUN, MALEKUN SALA.
(I give you thanks and praise).

I call the Congo Spirits from the North.
I call the Congo Spirits from the South.
I call the Congo Spirits from the East.
I call the Congo Spirits from the West.

I am here, (say your complete birth name).

I summon you to come from where you are from your world to my world. Place a ring of protective light around my body so that my enemies known and unknown will not see me nor hear what is about to be revealed to me here at this sacred ceremony.

O powerful and mighty Congo Spirits, your enemies are my enemies and my enemies are your enemies. I have brought you light, so that that you will light my roads in darkness. I ask you in the name of Divine justice that you bring back all of the good things that were taken from me by my enemies be returned back to my hands.

O powerful and mighty Congo Spirits, we stand here together to fight a common enemy.

O powerful and mighty Congo Spirits, I call upon the Congo Spirit, Lucero to open up the doors of communication to your world and to my world.

O powerful and mighty Congo Spirits, by the power of Nzambi, the God of the great Heavens and of the Earth, I cause this sacred ritual into being.

SALA MALEKUN, MALEKUN SALA.
(I give you thanks and praise).

O powerful and mighty Congo Spirits, whatever my enemies have done to me in the past, are presently doing or plan to do to me in the future, I ask that you punish them 9 x 9 x 9 and bring them to their knees, so that they will relinquish any hold that they may have over me.

O powerful and mighty Congo Spirits, I ask that you break my enemies.

O powerful and mighty Congo Spirits, I ask that you blind my enemies.

O powerful and mighty Congo Spirits, I ask that you bind my enemies.

O powerful and mighty Congo Spirits, I ask that you destroy my enemies.

In the name of the great force which binds man to the great cosmos, I ask that if it be your will, so may it be done on Earth as it is in Heaven.

SALA MALEKUN, MALEKUN SALA.
(I give you thanks and praise).

LUCERO BRILLUMBI NDOKI INFIERNO VIRA MUNDO.
(Spirit Lucero, it is you who lights and turns the World).

KOBAYENDE BRILLUMBI NDOKI INFIERNO VIRA MUNDO.
(Spirit Kobayende, it is you who lights and turns the World).

CENTELLA NDOKI BRILLUMBI NDOKI INFIERNO VIRA MUNDO.
(Spirit Centella Ndoki, it is you who lights and turns the World).

GURUNFINDA BRILLUMBI NDOKI INFIERNO VIRA MUNDO.
(Spirit Gurunfina, it is you who lights and turns the World).

MADRE DE AGUA BRILLUMBI NDOKI INFIERNO VIRA MUNDO.
(Spirit Madre De Agua, it is you who lights and turns the World).

CALUNGA BRILLUMBI NDOKI INFIERNO VIRA MUNDO.
(Spirit Calunga, it is you who lights and turns the World).

MAMA SHOLAN BRILLUMBI NDOKI INFIERNO VIRA MUNDO.
(Spirit Mama Sholan, it is you who lights and turns the World).

TIEMPO VIEJO BRILLUMBI NDOKI INFIERNO VIRA MUNDO.
(Spirit Tiempo Viejo, it is you who lights and turns the World).

CABO RONDO BRILLUMBI NDOKI INFIERNO VIRA MUNDO.
(Spirit Cabo Rondo, it is you who lights and turns the World).

SIETE RAYOS BRILLUMBI NDOKI INFIERNO VIRA MUNDO.
(Spirit Siete Rayos, it is you who lights and turns the World).

TIEMBLA TIERRA BRILLUMBI NDOKI INFIERNO VIRA MUNDO.
(Spirit Tiembla Tierra, it is you who lights and turns the World).

ZARABANDA BRILLUMBI NDOKI INFIERNO VIRA MUNDO.
(Spirit Zarabanda, it is you who lights and turns the World).

BRAZO FUERTE BRILLUMBI NDOKI INFIERNO VIRA MUNDO.
(Spirit Brazo Fuerte, it is you who lights and turns the World).

NSAMBA NTALA BRILLUMBI NDOKI INFIERNO VIRA MUNDO.
(Spirit Nsamba Ntala, it is you who lights and turns the World).

WHO IS THE GREATEST IN HEAVEN*?* *NZAMBI*
WHO IS THE GREATEST IN HEAVEN*?* *NZAMBI*
WHO IS THE GREATEST IN HEAVEN*?* *NZAMBI*
WHO ARE YOU*?*
WHO ARE YOU*?*
WHO ARE YOU*?*

SALA MALEKUN, MALEKUN SALA.
(I give you thanks and praise).

8. After reciting this opening sacred ritual prayer, place a chair within the circle directly in front of the Spiritual cauldron and sit in it. Remain siting in the chair while meditating upon your desires for 30 minutes to 1 hour.

This is a very good ritual to practice if you want to increase your spiritual connection with your spirit guides which reside in the Spiritual Cauldron. By frequently doing this ritual you will start to see fast spiritual results. This ritual can also be done directly in front of your Spiritual Boveda.

HOW TO MAKE THE SACRED SPIRIT OMIERO

The sacred herbal liquid drink of the spirits is known as omiero. Omiero is a specially prepared drink which is believed to have magical properties. Every spirit has their own sacred omiero attributed to them.

Omiero is prepared with a variety of ingredients such as rain water, sea water, palm oil, cascarilla, honey and a variety of herbs. Omiero is used in all of the ceremonies and rituals. Omiero is used for such things as to consecrate the sacred beads (collares), chamalongo divination shells, amulets and to feed the matarib sacred spirit stones). Omiero is also used by initiates as medicine. Omiero has been known to heal disease and spiritual sickness.

The number of fresh herbs used in the preparation of the omiero depends on the particular spirit being invokes and prepared. The following is a chart for the number of herbs attributed to each of the major Congo Spirit deities.

GENERAL OMIERO *- 21 OR 121 HERBS*

LUCERO OMIERO *- 21 OR 121 HERBS*

EGGUN OMIERO *- 9, 21 OR 121 HERBS*

CENTELLE NDOKI OMIERO *- 9 HERBS*

ZARABANDA OMIERO *- 9 HERBS*

TIEMBLA TIERRA OMIERO *- 8 HERBS*

MADRE DE AGUA OMIERO *- 7 HERBS*

MAMA SHOLAN OMIERO *- 5 HERBS*

CABO RONDO OMIERO *- 7 HERBS*

PRENDA JUDIA OMIERO - 9, *21, 121 HERBS*

OZAIN OMIERO - *21 OR 121 HERBS*

BRAZO FUERTE OMIERO - *6 HERBS*

SIETE RAYOS OMIERO - *6 or 7 HERBS*

KOBAYENDE OMIERO - *16 HERBS*

NSAMBA NTALA OMIERO - *2, 4 OR 21 HERBS*

AJE SPIRITS OMIERO - *9, 21 OR 121 HERBS*

ITEMS NECESSARY TO PREPARE THE OMIERO

1. *ONE LARGE BOWL*
2. *TWENTY-ONE GRAINS OF PARADISE*
3. *BEE'S HONEY*
4. *POWDERED SMOKED FISH*
5. *POWDERED SMOKED JUTIA*
6. *CIGARS*
7. *RUM*
8. *(4) PIECES OF PREPARED COCONUTS FOR DIVINATION*
9. *ONE STRAW MAT (ESTERA)*
10. *PEMBA*
11. *FRESH HERBS*
12. *FRESH WATER*
13. *HOLY WATER*
14. *MAY RAIN WATER*
15. *COCONUT WATER*

(HOLY WATER FROM A CHURCH IS OPTIONAL)

PREPARATION

1. Lay the straw mat on the floor.

2. Place the large bowl which you will be preparing the Omiero into the center of the straw mat.

3. Pour all of the waters into the bowl.

4. Place all of the herbs on the mat.

5. Spray the herbs with rum and blow the smoke from a cigar over all of the herbs.

6. Place all of the items which you will be using to prepare the omiero on the mat.

7. Light a white candle and place it next to the bowl.

8. Pick up all of the herbs in both of your hands and hold them up to the sky and say and do the following:

CON LA BENDICION Y LA LICENCIA DE NSAMBI,

SALA MALEKUN, MALEKUN SALA

CON LA BENDICION Y LA LICENCIA DE EGGUN,

SALA MALEKUN, MALEKUN SALA

CON LA BENDICION Y LA LICENCIA DE LUCERO - SALA MALEKUN, MALEKUN SALA

CON LA BENDICION Y LA LICENCIA DE OZAIN - SALA MALEKUN, MALEKUN SALA

CON LA BENDICION Y LA LICENCIA DE - SAY THE NAME OF THE SPIRIT - SALA MALEKUN, MALEKUN SALA

9. After saying the above prayer, kiss the herbs in your hands three times and then begin to pull off all of the leaves and place them into the bowl.

10. Sitting in a chair in front of the bowl, begin ripping and tearing the herbs in the waters. This is called making *"Ozain."*

11. Sing the following mambo while making the omiero:

KAMA MA IYA - IYA IYA
KAMA MA ENU - ENU ENU
KAMA MA EBO - EBO EBO
KAMA MA EPO - EPO EPO
MA MA MA IYA IYA IYA.
MA MA MA IYA IYA IYA.
MA MA MA IYA IYA IYA.
EBO EBO EBO EBO EBO
EBO EBO EBO EBO EBO
EWE EWE EWE EWE EWE
EWE EWE EWE EWE EWE
MA MA MA IYA IYA IYA.
MA MA MA IYA IYA IYA.
MA MA MA IYA IYA IYA.
EBO EBO EBO EBO EBO
EBO EBO EBO EBO EBO
EWE EWE EWE EWE EWE
EWE EWE EWE EWE EWE

REPEAT THIS SONG UNTIL YOU HAVE FINISHED PREPARING THE OMIERO.

12. When you have finished, add the following items into the omiero liquid; honey, grains of paradise, smoked fish and jutia.

13. Check with the four coconut pieces in the divination ritual to see if the omiero has been prepared correctly.

14. If the answer comes with a yes then drip candle wax into the omiero liquid. The amount of drops will depend on the spirit omiero being prepared. Use the chart on the first page of this chapter. (For example if the omiero is for the Spirit Zarabanda then place 9 drops of candle wax into the omiero)

THE CANDLE WAX SEALS THE MAGICAL POWER (ACHE) OF HERBS INTO THE SACRED OMIERO.

HOW TO PREPARE THE SPIRIT BEADS

Items Necessary

1. ONE STRAND OF MULTICOLORED BEADS
2. OMIERO OF THE SPIRIT
3. HONEY
4. RUM
5. RED WINE
6. ONE WHITE CANDLE
7. ONE RED CANDLE
8. ONE BLACK CANDLE

Preparation of the Spirit Beads

1. Place a large bowl of Omiero in front of the Spiritual Cauldron. 2. Place the strand of beads into the Omiero. 3. Light all of the candles and place them next to the bowl. 4. Invoke the spirit. 5. Pour honey and red wine over the spirits and into the bowl containing the spirit beads. 6. Allow the beads to soak for a 24 hour period of time. After the 24 hours remove the beads and clean using rum and by blowing cigar smoke over them. 7. Place the beads into the Spiritual Cauldron allowing them to become energized with the powerful energy of the spirits before presenting them to an individual.

TRADITIONAL CONGO MAMBOS

The following traditional Congo songs (Mambos) are used in the Afro-Caribbean religion known as Palo Mayombe. All of the following Congo Mambos can be used and sung in the preparation of the Spiritual Cauldron or during religious ceremonies.

SALA MALEKUN - MALEKUN SALA

Group;
Sala male male, sala male, malekun sala

Leader;
Ay que yo jura, yo jura en kisi, sala malekun, malekun,

Group;
Sala male male, sala male, malekun sala

Leader;
Ay que yo jura, yo jura menga, sala malekun, malekun,

Group;
Sala male male, sala male, malekun sala

Leader;
Ay que yo jura, yo jura en nganga, sala malekun, malekun,

Group;
Sala male male, sala male, malekun sala

Leader;
Yo jura, yo jura en fumbi, sala malekun, malekun,

Group;
Sala male male, sala male, malekun sala

Leader;

Yo saludo a Nsambi, sala malekun, malekun sala,

Group;

Sala male male, sala male, malekun sala

Leader;

Yo saludo a Eggun, sala malekun, malecun sala,

Group;

Sala male male, sala male, malekun sala

Leader;

Yo saludo a Lucerito, sala malekun, malekun sala

Group;

Sala male male, sala male, malekun sala

Leader;

Yo saludo a Tiembla Tierra, sala malekun, malekun sala.

Group;

Sala male male, sala male, malekun sala

Leader;

Yo saludo a Zarabanda, sala malekun, malekun sala.

Group;

Sala male male, sala male, malekun sala 140

Leader;

Yo saludo a Cabo Rondo, sala malekun, malekun sala.

Group;

Sala male male, sala male, malekun sala

Leader;

Yo saludo a Siete Rayos, sala malekun, malekun sala.

Group;

Sala male male, sala male, malekun sala

Leader;

Yo saludo a Madre De Agua, sala male, malekun sala.

Group;

Sala male male, sala male, malekun sala

Leader;

Yo saludo a Sholan Guengue, sala malekun, malekun sala.

Group;

Sala male male, sala male, malekun sala

Leader;

Yo saludo a Brazo Fuerte, sala malekun, malekun sala.

Group;

Sala male male, sala male, malekun sala

Leader;

Yo saludo a Centelle Ndoki, sala malekun, malekun sala.

Group;

Sala male male, sala male, malekun sala

Leader;

Yo saludo a Nsamba Ntala, sala malekun, malekun sala.

Group;

Sala male male, sala male, malekun sala

Leader;

Yo saludo a Kobayende, sala malekun, malekun sala.

Group;
Sala male male, sala male, malekun sala

Leader;
Ay que yo jura, yo jura en kisa, sala malekun, malekun,

Group;
Sala male male, sala male, malekun sala

Leader;
Ay que yo jura, yo jura en kisa, sala malekun, malekun,

Group;
Sala male male, sala male, malekun sala

Leader;
Ay que yo jura, yo jura en kisa, sala malekun, malekun,

Group;
Sala male male, sala male, malekun sala

Leader;
Ay que yo jura, yo jura en kisa, sala malekun, malekun,

Group;
Sala male male, sala male, malekun sala

Leader;
Ay que yo jura, yo jura en kisa, sala malekun, malekun,

SALA MALE, MALE, MALEKUN SALA
SALA MALE, MALE, MALEKUN SALA
SALA MALE, MALE, MALEKUN SALA

LA BUENA NOCHE AQUI - LA BUENA NOCHE ALLA

Leader;

La Buena Noche aqui
La Buena Noche Alla
Sala Malekun Aqui
Sala Malekun Alla

Group;

La Buena Noche aqui
La Buena Noche Alla
Sala Malekun Aqui
Sala Malekun Alla

Leader;

La Buena Noche aqui
La Buena Noche Alla
Sala Malekun Aqui
Sala Malekun Alla

Group;

La Buena Noche aqui
La Buena Noche Alla
Sala Malekun Aqui 142
Sala Malekun Alla

Leader;

La Buena Noche aqui
La Buena Noche Alla
Sala Malekun Aqui
Sala Malekun Alla

Group;

La Buena Noche aqui
La Buena Noche Alla
Sala Malekun Aqui
Sala Malekun Alla
Sala Malekun Aqui
Sala Malekun Alla
La Buena Noche Aqui
La Buena Noche Alla

TO ATTRACT MONEY

Boil all of the following herbs together in hot water; Abre Camno Herb, Para Mi Herb, Ven A Mi Herb, Cinnamon Powder, Amansa Guapo Herb. After the herbs have come to a full boil allow the liquid to cool. After the liquid cools, strain the liquid into another container and add Florida Water, Orange Water and some of your favorite perfume or cologne. Pour the liquid mixture into a warm bath and light a green candle. Do this spiritual bath for three consecutive days.

TO ATTRACT SUCCESS

Make a candle dressing using the following ingredients; Abre Camino Herb Powder, Jala Jala Herb Powder, Ven A Mi Herb Powder and Precipitado Rojo. Dress a yellow candle and burn it for seven consecutive days.

TO ATTRACT CLIENTS TO A BUSINESS

Mix together the following ingredients and sprinkle around your business daily for fast business success. (Abre Camino Herb Powder, Ven A Mi Herb Powder, Jala Jala Herb Powder, Vence Batalla Herb Powder, Deer Horn Powder.

TO REMOVE WITCHCRAFT

Draw the Spirit Signature of the Congo Spirit Lucero at your front door. Place a white candle into the center of it and then light it. Blow cigar smoke over the spirit signature and all over the front door. Spray rum directly on the spirit signature and all over the front door. Place a glass of fresh water next to the candle. feed the spirit signature the blood from a rooster. Using the blood of the rooster take your fingers and mark the four corners of the front door with the blood. Pour bee's honey over the spirit signature. Leave the spirit offering there for at least 24 hours before cleaning it up. A very good spiritual work to remove witchcraft that your enemies may have sent to your home by dropping it off at your front door.

TO ATTRACT AN INDIVIDUAL TO YOU FOR ROMANCE

Write the name of the desired individual on a piece of brown paper three times across it. Place the paper on a white plate facing up. Sprinkle the following ingredients on top of the paper; Palo Amansa Guapo Powder, Cinnamon Powder, Nutmeg Powder, Precipitado Rojo Powder, Spider Powder, Domination Palo. Pour Bee's honey over all of these ingredients and over the top of the brown paper. Place the white plate with the spiritual work on it directly in front of the Congo Spirit Lucero. Light three red candles in front of the Spirit Lucero daily for three consecutive days. After the three days place the remains from the spiritual offering into a brown paper bag along with 21 pennies and leave it next to the crossroads close to your home.

TO BANISH SICKNESS

Draw the Spirit Signature of the Spirit Kobayende with purple paint on a white plate. Place a picture of the sick individual into the center of the plate and on top of the Spirit Signature. Place a seven day glass religious candle into the center of the plate and directly on top of the picture and the Spirit Signature. Pour Palm oil onto the plate around the base of the glass candle with honey. Invoke the Congo Kobayende for seven consecutive days. After the seven days take the entire offering to the crossroads near a hospital and leave it there with 9 pennies.

TO BANISH NEGATIVE VIBRATION

Take a spiritual bath for three consecutive days using the following herbs; Basil, Rompezaraguey, Siempre Viva, Quita Maldicion and Mint. During the three days that you take your spiritual bath light a white candle and offer it to your Guardian Angel. Place a glass of fresh water next to the candle and dispose of the water after the three days.

TO FIND FAST EMPLOYMENT

Take a spiritual bath for three consecutive days using the 21 herbs sacred to the Congo Spirit Lucero. Light a green Bayberry candle.

TO CAUSE CONFLICTS BETWEEN TWO INDIVIDUALS

Write the names of the two individuals on a piece of brown paper nine times each so they cross over each other in the form of a cross. Wrap the paper around a small piece of Palo Cambia Rumbo and wrap it using a black thread. Place the prepared item into a glass jar with the following ingredients; White Vinegar, Conflict Powder, African frog Powder, Precipitado Rojo, Spider Powder, Black Coffee Grounds, Used Car Oil and a small amount of Milk. Bury the glass jar in the individual's yard.

TO MAKE A LOST LOVE RETURN TO YOU

Write the name of the individual that you desire to return to you on a piece of brown paper. Place the paper into a tin can along with the following ingredients; Para Mi Powder, Ven A Mi Powder, Jala Jala Powder and Amansa Guapo Powder. Place two small feathers from a Vulture in the form of a cross and set it on top of the other ingredients in the tin can. Light all of the ingredients on fire and burn it by your front door reciting the following prayer to the Congo Spirit Mama Chola; Sala Malekun, Malekun Sala, Divine Mother Mama Chola, Goddess of love and all of the sweet things in life, Bring me (say the name of the individual) to me without delay on their hands and knees. Do this ritual for three consecutive nights beginning at 12 midnight.

TO MAKE AN INDIVIDUAL CALL YOU

Prepare and dress a pink candle using the following ingredients; Jala Jala oil, Ven A Mi oil, Yo Puedo Mas Que Tu oil, Amansa Guapo oil, Cinnamon Powder, Nutmeg Powder and Clove Powder. After the candle has been prepared, place it on top of the picture of the individual and light the candle calling out the name of the person seven times to come to you out loud.

TO BRING GAMBLING SUCCESS

Prepare and dress a green candle using the following ingredients; Jala Jala oil, Ven A Mi oil, Para Mi oil, Hair from your head in powdered form, A dried Four Leaf Clover, Precipitado Rojo and Deer horn Powder. Burn the candle for three consecutive days before you go out to gamble.

THE CONGO SPIRIT SIGNATURES

In Congo magic, spirit signature sigils (seals) are symbols connected to a set of ideas by which spirits or deities may be summoned to awareness and controlled. The spirit signature sigils connect the spirits to our earthly realm. The spirit signature sigils when used in the appropriate magical manner open up the doors to world of the supernatural. They are used in divinatory practices. In Spanish they are called "*Firmas*" which means signature. The spirit signature sigil itself when drawn out on the ground or drawn on an object will call forth the spirit. The spirit signature sigil also serves as a physical focus through which the Congo magician achieves the desired state of mind. Spirit signature sigils represent the secret names of spirits and deities who manifest themselves differently to each magic practitioner. Once the Congo magician has summoned the spirit or deity he may control it, if necessary, by subjecting its sigil to fire or the use of a magical sword or machete. Spirit signature sigils can also serve as amulets, talismans, or meditation tools. Congo spirit signature sigils may be of various signs, such as crosses, tridents, stars associated with different deities. Some of the best spirit sigils are attained through intuition and inspiration. Many come through meditation and the practice of scrying; when a certain pattern seems to appear upon the object which the individual is gazing at. Others believe symbols are occasionally mystically produced when asked for. Congo magicians often times inscribe the spirit signature sigil on ceremonial ritual objects, candles or objects of silver, brass, gold, or glass. Such spirit signatures sigils are considered to be magically powerful. Congo magicians also draw these very sacred and powerful spirit signature sigils directly on the ground in front of the Congo spirit nganga to invoke and to summon the deities to appear and to send them to do their bidding. The following Congo Spirit Signature Sigils (Firmas) can be used when making a spirit nganga, amulets, macuttos, candles, spells and rituals.

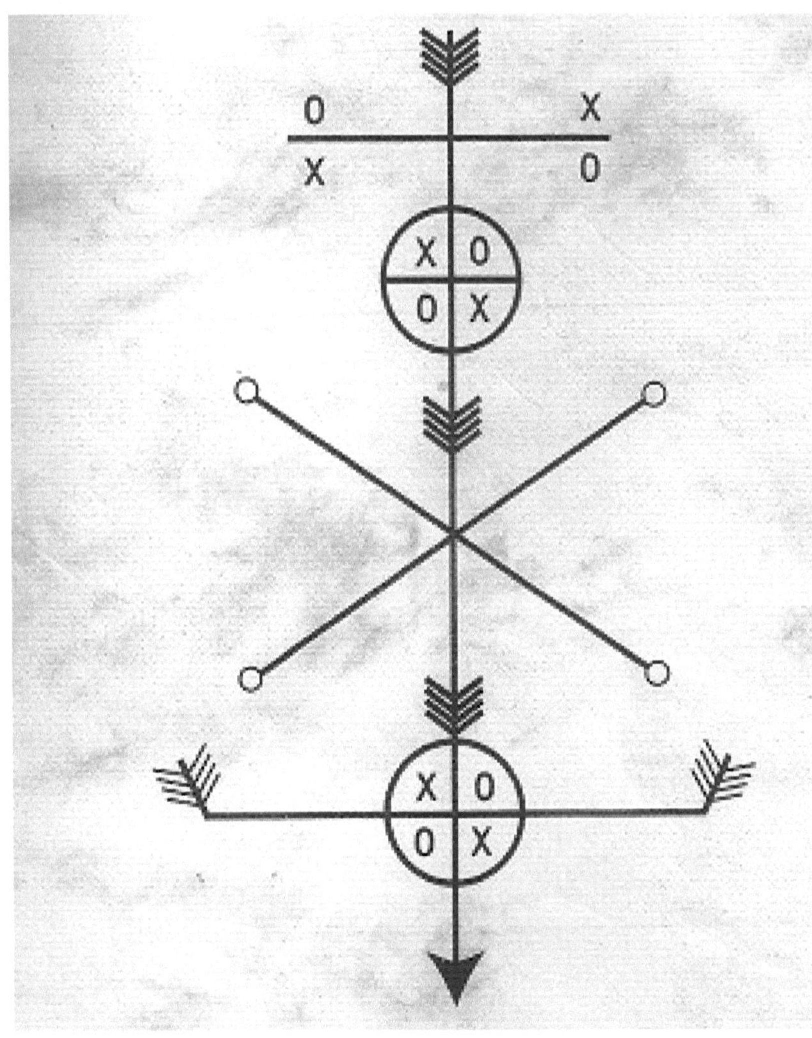

SPIRIT SIGNATURE OF NZAMBI

SPIRIT SIGNATURE OF LUCERO

SPIRIT SIGNATURE OF KOBAYENDE

SPIRIT SIGNATURE OF CENTELLA NDOKI

SPIRIT SIGNATURE OF GURUNFINDA

SPIRIT SIGNATURE OF MADRE DE AGUA

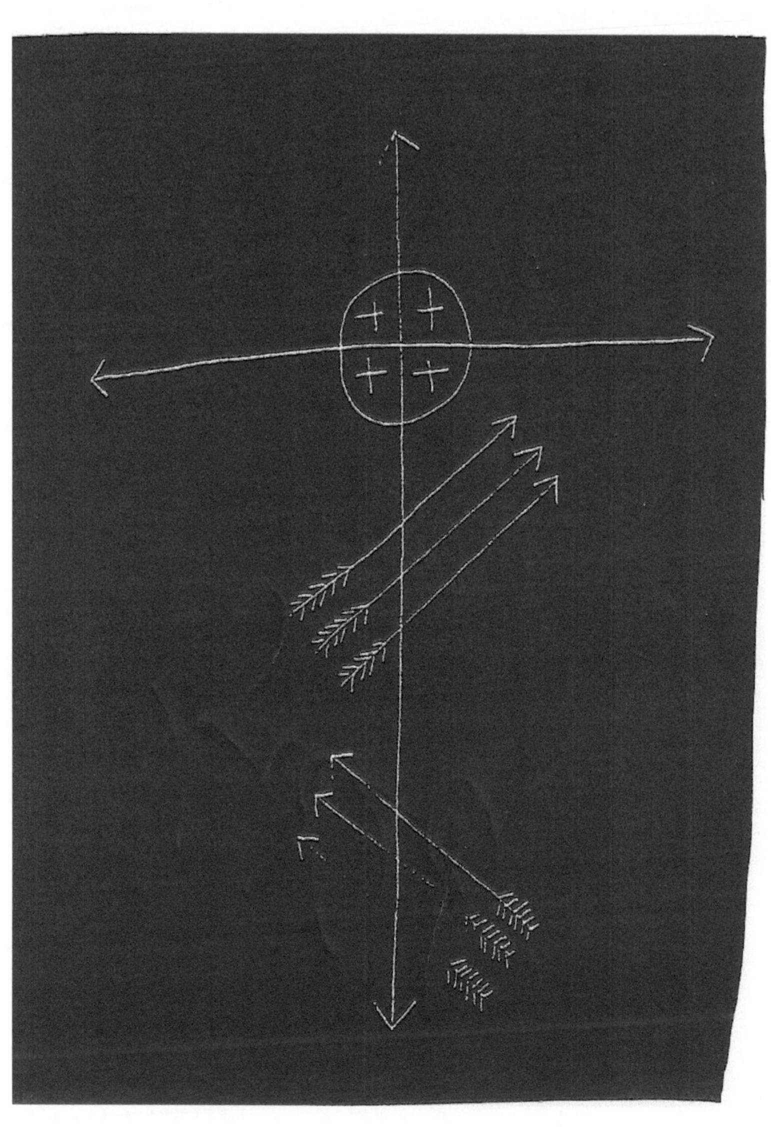

SPIRIT SIGNATURE OF CALUNGA

SPIRIT SIGNATURE OF MAMA SHOLAN

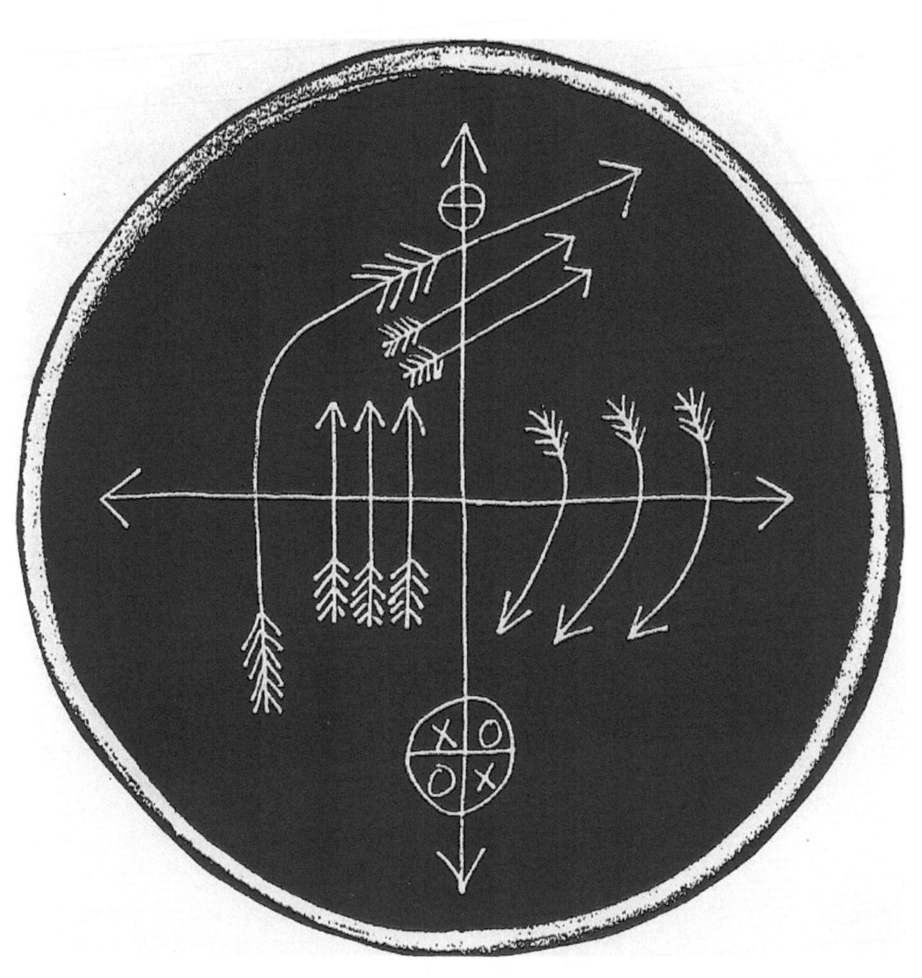

SPIRIT SIGNATURE OF TIEMPO VIEJO

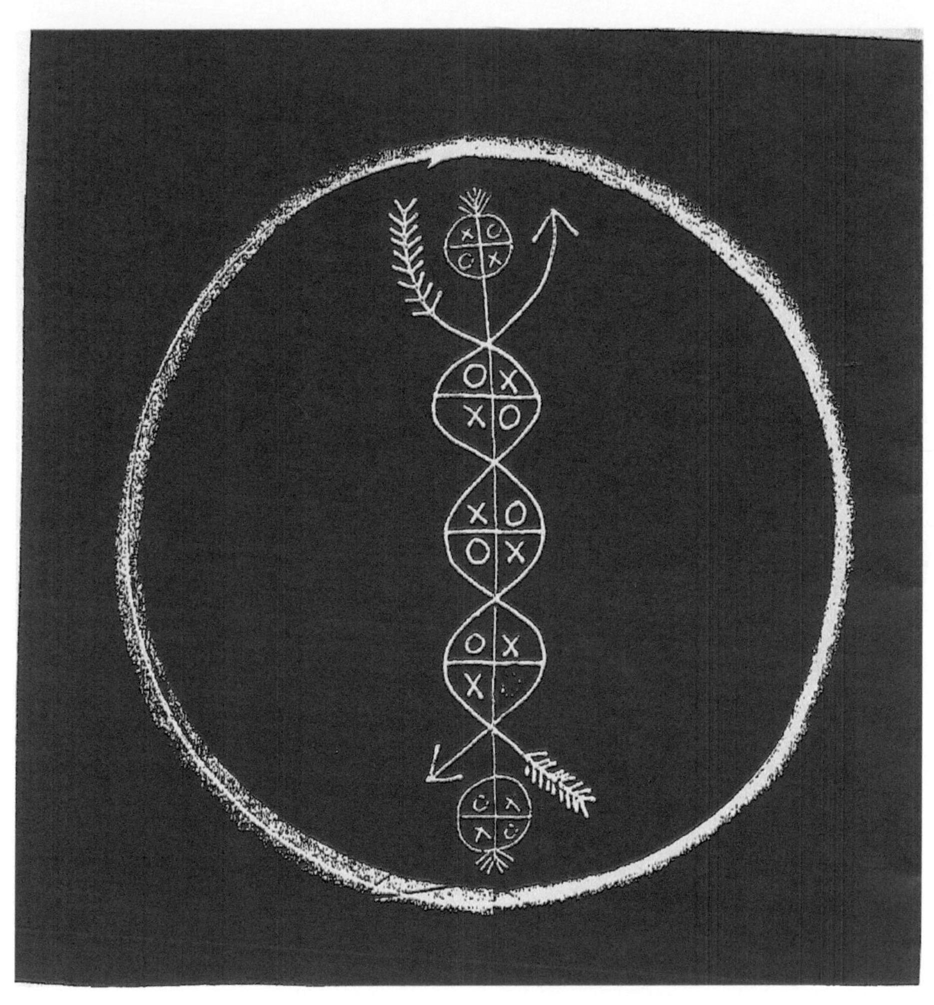

SIGNATURE OF CABO RONDO

SPIRIT SIGNATURE OF SIETE RAYOS

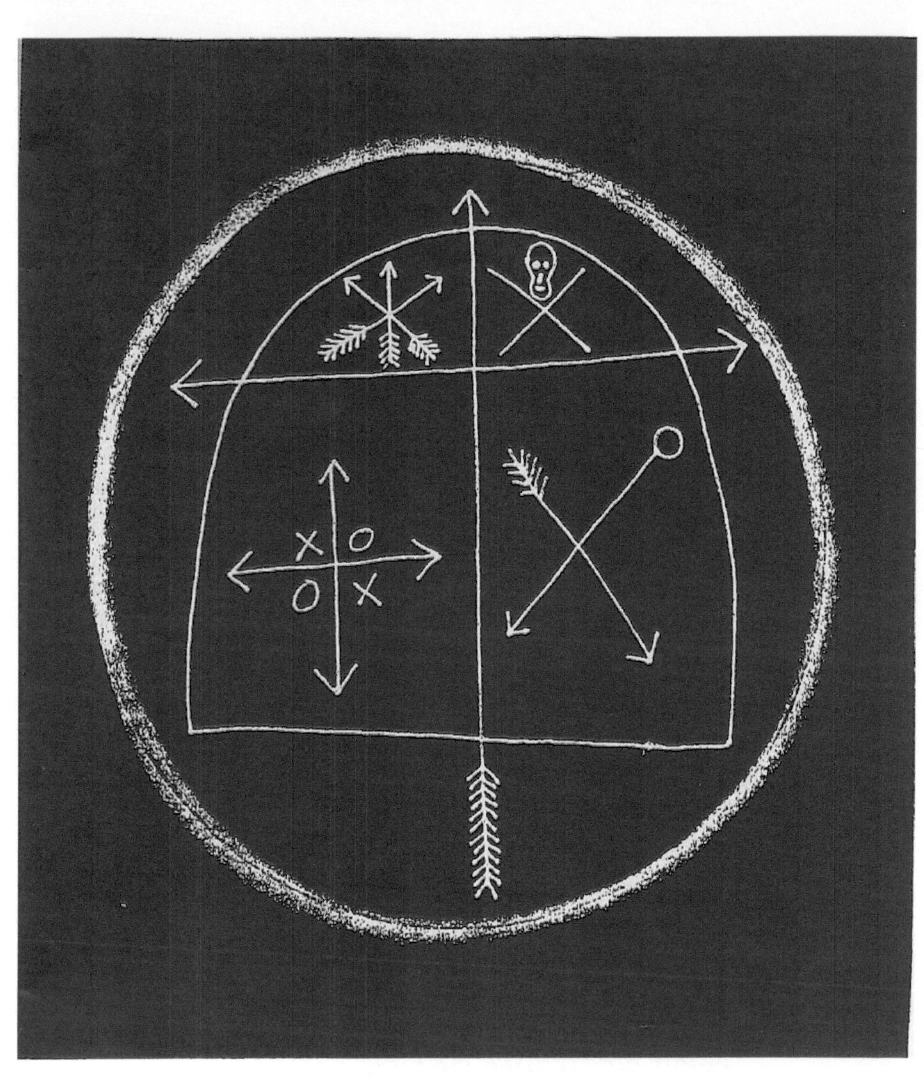

SPIRIT SIGNATURE OF TIEMBLA TIERRA

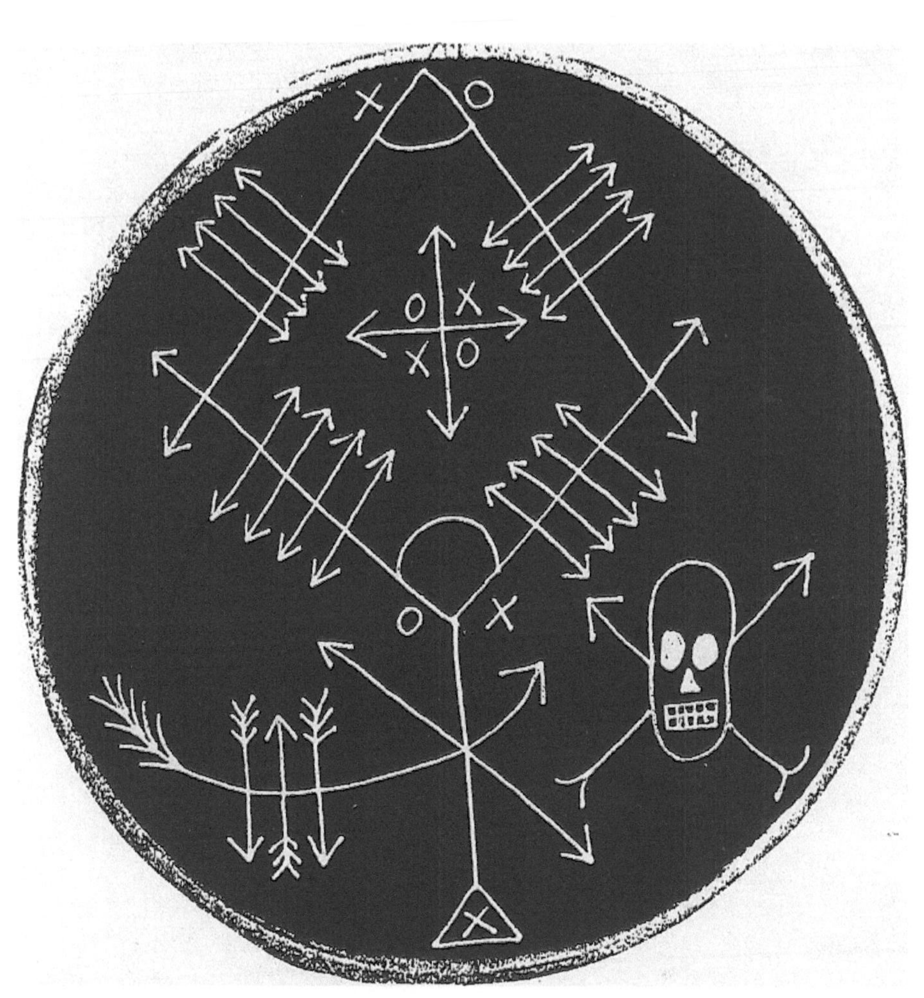

SPIRIT SIGNATURE OF ZARABANDA

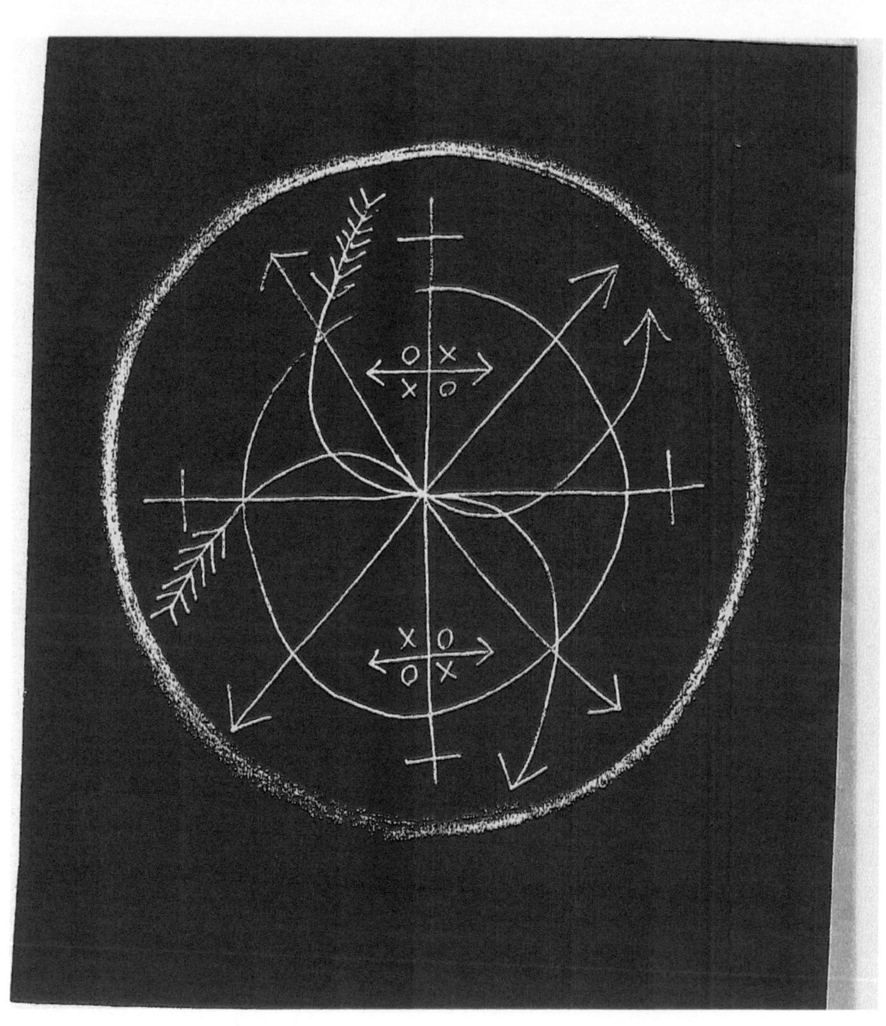

SPIRIT SIGNATURE OF BRAZO FUERTE

SPIRIT SIGNATURE OF NSAMBA NTALA

SPIRIT SIGNATURE OF THE EGGUN SPIRITS

SPIRIT SIGNATURE OF THE SPIRITUAL CAULDRON (CALDERO ESPIRITUAL). THIS MAGICAL SIGIL CAN BE PAINTED USING WHITE PAINT ON THE INSIDE BOTTOM OF THE IRON POT WHICH WILL BE HOUSING THESE SPIRIT MYSTERIES. PAINTING THIS SPIRIT SIGNATURE IS OPTIONAL.

www.ingramcontent.com/pod-product-compliance
Ingram Content Group UK Ltd.
Pitfield, Milton Keynes, MK11 3LW, UK
UKHW041927190726
13854UKWH00003B/1483